M000202497

ELEMENTARY
TEACHINGS OF ISLAM

By

Moulana Mohammed Abdul-Aleem Siddiqui

KAZI PUBLICATIONS INC.
3023 West Belmont Avenue
Chicago, IL 60618 (U.S.A.)

Library of Congress Cataloging in Publication Data
Muhammad Abdul Aleem Siddiqui
    Elementary Teachings of Islam
    1. Islam—Juvenile literature
    1. Title   II. Islam for children 9-15
    297 BP161.2

ISBN: 0-935782-89-3

Publisher:

Library of Islam
P. O. Box 595
South Elgin IL 60177

Distributor:

KAZI Publications, Inc.
3023 West Belmont Avenue
Chicago IL 60618
Tel: 312-267-7001

CONTENTS

PART I

PART II

بِسْمِ اللهِ الرَّحْمٰنِ الرَّحِيمِ

نَحْمَدُهُ وَ نُصَلِّىْ عَلَى رَسُوْلِهِ الْكَرِيْمِ

PREFACE TO THE THIRD EDITION

It is a living miracle of the Truth of Islam that, though it has neither a backing of huge missionary corporations, nor does it have any authentic literature in foreign languages, yet people after people, attracted to it by its inherent, magnetic force, keep on embracing this religion of love and universal brotherhood. For, whenever either by dint of personal research and study or by a chance-contact with, and the consequent guidance of a real Muslim theologian they learn the true facts about Islam, the invariable conclusion they arrive at is that Islam is a very simple religion and all its teachings are perfectly rational and in complete consonance with the laws of nature.

It is not a new religion, but a divinely-executed combination of all the old inspired ones and provides the via media, the golden means. On the one hand, its comprehensively high code of ethics, which is unique for many reasons, equips its votary of his journey towards the ultimate goal of a sincere seeker after Truth—Allah, and on the other directs its followers to foster and maintain fraternal relations with all the human beings and achieve the utmost progress in all the spheres of art and science and the material walks of life.

This is the only religion, the Sacred Book of which, the Holy Qur'an, is preserved intact in its pristine purity and an authentic record of the minutest details and the eventful life of its promulgator, Prophet Muhammad (May peace and blessings of Allah be on him), is extant to this day after a lapse of more than thirteen centuries.

The necessity of the presentation of the elementary teachings of Islam, explaining its Cardinal Articles of Faith and the Fundamental Principles in the simplest possible English language is therefore, obvious; for such a publication would not only serve to acquaint the English-knowing new Muslims with the essentials of Faith and the directions for engaging in devotion to Allah, but also supply the long-felt need of a handy book for imparting the rudiments of Islam to the Muslim children of those countries where the English Language rules supreme and children are sent away to school using English as medium of instruction, without having any knowledge, whatsoever, of their religion.

Realising the urgency of publishing such a volume, I, during my itinerary of Ceylon, Singapore, Penang, Java, etc., drafted out a skeleton

i

according to the Shafi'i School in spite of numerous pre-occupations. My learned friend, Mr. M.I.M. Haniffa, B.A. (London), Advocate of Colombo, very kindly undertook to revise and touch it up and it was due to his invaluable assistance that "A Short Catechism of the First Teachings of Islam" was published a few years ago, and has proved very beneficial.

About the same time an incomplete and imperfect draft, according to the Hanafi School, was released for publication in "The Real Islam" of Singapore on account of pressing demands. The present volume is a thoroughly revised and enlarged edition of that draft. While sending it to the press I feel, I must knowledge the co-operation, in this humble work, of Mr. K.S. Anwari, my Secretary, during the South and East African tour, and of my son-in-law Hafiz Muhammad Fazlur Rahman Ansari, B.A. (Alig.).

While expressing the hope that this little volume will serve the purpose in view and will meet the approval of all those concerned, I desire to record my sincere thanks to Al-Haj Mohammad Ibrahim of Trinidad for liberally undertaking the cost of printing and thus rendering a signal service to Islam and to the public.

If it pleases Allah, a second volume, in which commonsense arguments in support of the Cardinal Articles of Faith and a much more detailed treatment of the Principles of Islam and the laws governing society will be incorporated, will soon follow this modest attempt.

May it please Allah to accept this humble service. Amen!

MOHAMMED ABDUL ALEEM SIDDIQUI.
268 Mashaikhan Street,
Meerut City (India).

THE PRINCIPLES OF ISLAM

I

Know, child, that God is only one,
And has no Partner or Son;
He has made us and everything,
All beasts, all fowls, all birds that sing,
The Sun, the Moon, the Starry Sky,
The land, the sea, the mountains high.
He knows whate'er we think or act,
By Him is seen the real fact.
And only He does what He wills,
He makes, He keeps, He saves, His kills.
Fore'er the same, no age, no youth,
He is Perfection, He is Truth.
Almighty, All-seeing, Wise,
He hath not form or shape or size.
But Self-existing is our Lord,
And is always to be adored.

II

Our God is Just, and loves the right,
The wrong is hateful to His sight.
To all His creatures He is Kind,
He gave us reason that we might
Know good from bad wrong from right.
This is the first to light our path,
To gain His grace and shun His wrath.
But gift of reason varies far,
Some wise and others foolish are.
The eyes of mind our passion dims,
And reason oft is quenched by whims.
For second guide we have the men
Of larger mind and wider ken,
Who could from God a message get,
His Law before the people set.
We call them Prophets, know you well,

1

Coming events they could foretell.
No nation was without such guide,
To warn them and from sins to chide.
Each Prophet taught in his own sphere,
To worship God and Him to fear.
But thousands of such Prophets came,
Of whom we know not the name,
Of some well-known I mention make,
The Lord God bless us for their sake!
Job, Jacob, Joseph, Abraham,
Elias, David, Solomon,
Lot, Moses, Aaron, Ishmael,
Hod, Noah, Jesus, Daniel;
With Adam first and Muhammad last,
Between the two all others pass.
Their minds were brighter than our own.
But otherwise all flesh and bone;
God did not in them incorporate.
They were but men and separate.

IV

The Books of God, a third guide form,
And us of His Commands inform,
God sent them through His Prophets Great,
Repealing Older by the Late;
The Qur'an now the law in force,
The other Books have run their course.

V

In all these Books 'tis plainly said,
The graves will once give up their dead;
A new life God will give to men.
Who made us once will quicken again.
That day we shall, to judgment brought,
Be called to answer what we wrought,
And shall be judged by Faith we had,
And work we did good or bad.

The good shall get a festive treat—
Everlasting bliss and heavenly seat,
Where such the pleasure, such the mirth,
We've never dreamt of on this earth.
The bad shall go to hell and fire,
And suffer pains and torture dire.
But sense of guilt to conscious mind
Is more than all the pains combined
While sense of having pleased our Lord
Is greatest bliss and highest reward.

VI

The Qur'an teaches us to pray
Our Lord God five times a day;
To fast the days of Ramadan lent,
To give alms to the indigent;
To visit Mecca once in life,
And to make for God every strife.
Find here the Muslim Laws in brief,
May God guide all to this belief.

—*Sayyed Mohammad*

THE PROPHET OF ISLAM

The crown of creation set with richest gems,
Diamonds and rubies in value beyond ken,
Unequalled in brilliance, unique of kind.
Art thou, O Great Prophet! to all mankind.
Truthful by nature and of most saintly mien,
All called thee the Trusty, the Al-Ameen.
Most loving to children, courteous to all,
To animals, tender, alike to great and small;
Never on earth a nobler soul has trod,
Never had another shewed a true way to God.

O sweetest flower that ever on earth did bloom,
Matchless alike in divine beauty and perfume,
O whitest lily that human eyes have seen,
O loveliest rose that in the world has been,
All nature join in homage, all men adore
Thee who brought light to a darksome world;
Thee whose teachings are as a necklace of pearls,
Which when worn does radiant beauty impart,
Adding lustre to body, to soul and to heart.
Ya Rasool-Allah! our dearest friend and guide,
May God's eternal blessings with thee abide.

From the Arabian deserts thou sounded thy call
To the worship of God, the Lord of all,
From the Arabian deserts thou taught mankind,
How the truest knowledge of God to find.
Thy words flew as lightning the whole world around,
Of Truth and Light they did fully abound,
And nations, acknowledging the pow'r of their sway,
Did find and follow the most truthful way.

In the wake of thy words true piety did spring,
And great knowledge and virtue did truly bring.
Never on earth a better soul was born,
Never the world did a purer soul adorn.

4

Man was fast sinking in idolatry and sin
When thou the great mission did first begin.
Then in place of darkness thou Light did give,
And taught mankind the noblest way to live;
And reformed the world as never before.
And unique blessings on it did bestow.
Praise be to Allah for this favour divine
In sending thee the wicked world to refine.
Search the world though we may from pole to pole
While the great ocean of time doth onward roll,
A more perfect Prophet never can we find,
Than thee who, thank God, gave Islam to mankind.
Ya Rasool-Allah! my homage I make to thee,
Ya Nabi-Allah! my love I tender thee,
My life, my all, for thee I gladly give,
Thy divine messages shall with me for ever live.
My love and thee no bounds doth know,
In my heart thy mem'ry shall every glow.
May Allah shower His choicest blessings on thee,
May Allah grant thee peace for all eternity.

M. J. MAJID,
Joint Secretary,
The Ceylon Muslim Missionary Society,
Colombo.

INTRODUCTORY CHAPTER

1. Q. **Who created you and all the worlds?**

A. Allah created me and all the worlds.

2. Q. **Who created Allah?**

A. Allah created us all. He is not created by anyone.

3. Q. **What are your duties to Allah (the Creator)?**

A. My duties to Allah are to have complete Faith (**Iman**) in Him and to submit myself entirely to His commands.

4. Q. **How can you have knowledge about Him and His commands?**

A. I can have knowledge about Him and His commands through His Apostles and Prophets.

5. Q. **WHat do you understand by an Apostle or a Prophet?**

A. An Apostle or a Prophet is a very true and pious man. He is chosen by Allah as His Messenger. Allah inspires him with His commands, and he conveys them to humanity. In this way, we may know the right path to lead a good life in this world and, thus pleasing Allah, may attain peace after death.

6. Q. **Were Prophets sent by Allah to all nations?**

A. Yes, Prophets were sent by Allah to all nations whenever and wherever there was a need for them. When all the nations were in need of one, Allah sent Prophet Muhammad for the whole world.

7. Q. **What did Prophet Muhammad teach you?**

A. Prophet Muhammad has taught me to render complete submission to the commands of Allah, which is called **Islam**.

8. Q. **What are the cardinal Articles of Faith in Islam?**

6

A. The cardinal Articles of Faith in Islam are seven in number, viz:—

(1) To believe in the oneness of Allah.

(2) To believe in all His Angels.

(3) To believe in all His Books.

(4) To believe in all His Prophets.

(5) To believe in the Day of Resurrection.

(6) To believe in the Day of Judgment.

(7) To believe that the power of doing all actions (whether good or bad) proceeds from Allah, but that we are responsible for our actions.

9. Q. What are the Fundamental Principles of Islam?

A. The Fundamental Principles of Islam are five in number, viz:—

(1) The declaration of **La ilaha illallah Muhammad-ur-rasoolul-lah,** meaning: There is no God but Allah, and Muhammad is His Prophet.

(2) The observance of the obligatory prayers five times a day.

(3) distribution of **Zakat** (Islamic alms-fee) among the deserving amounting to one fortieth in one's possession for a complete year.

(4) The observation of fasts during the day time in the month of Ramadan.

(5) The performance of **Hajj** (Pilgrimage) to Mecca, at least once in a lifetime, if circumstances permit.

PART I

Iman اِيْمَانْ

The Cardinal Articles of Faith in Islam

اٰمَنْتُ بِاللّٰهِ وَمَلٰٓئِكَتِهٖ وَكُتُبِهٖ وَرُسُلِهٖ وَالْيَوْمِ الْاٰخِرِ
وَالْقَدْرِ خَيْرِهٖ وَشَرِّهٖ مِنَ اللّٰهِ تَعَالٰى وَالْبَعْثِ
بَعْدَ الْمَوْتِ

9

CHAPTER I

ONENESS OF ALLAH

1. Q. What do you mean by belief in the Oneness of Allah?

A. By belief in the Oneness of Allah, I mean that Allah is one and that there is none like Him; He has no partner; He neither begets nor is He begotten; He is indivisible in person; He is eternal; He is infinite; He has neither beginning nor end; He is All-Mighty, the All-Knowing, the All-Just, the Cherisher of all worlds, the Patron, the Guide, the Helper, the Merciful, the Compassionate, etc.

2. Q. Where is Allah?

A. Allah is everywhere.

3. Q. Does Allah know all the actions you do on earth?

A. Certainly, Allah knows all the actions I do on earth, both good and bad. He even knows my secret thoughts.

4. Q. What has Allah done for you?

A. Allah has created me and all the worlds. He loves and cherishes me. He will reward me in Heaven for all my good actions and punish me in Hell for all my evil deeds.

5. Q. How can you win the love of Allah?

A. I can win the love of Allah by complete submission to His Will and obedience to His Commands.

6. Q. How can you know the Will and Commands of Allah?

A. I can know the will and Commands of Allah from the Holy Qur'an and from the Traditions of our Prophet Muhammad (May peace and blessing of Allah be upon him).

7. Q. **What is Iman (Faith)?**

A. **Iman** means "to believe in", i.e., to have a firm and sincere belief in the cardinal Articles of Faith.

8. Q. **What is Islam?**

A. **Islam** means "complete submission", i.e., submitting to the orders of Allah and acting in accordance with His Commands.

Note:—One who professes **Iman** is called a **Mu'min** (The Faithful), and one who observes all the principles of **Islam** is called a **Muslim**.

CHAPTER II

THE ANGELS OF ALLAH

1. Q. What kind of creatures are the Angels?

A. Angels are spiritual creatures of Allah, ever obedient to His Will and Commands. They are neither males nor females; they have neither parents, nor wives, nor husbands, nor sons, nor daughters. They have no material bodies, but can assume any form they like.

2. Q. Do Angels eat and drink like human beings?

A. Angels do not eat and drink like human beings, nor do they enjoy sleep.

3. Q. Can you name some of the most important Angels of Allah?

a. Yes, the most important Angels of Allah are four in number, viz.,

(1) Jibreel (جِبْرِيْلُ)

(2) Mika'il (مِيْكَاۤئِيْلُ)

(3) Israfeel (اِسْرَافِيْلُ)

(4) Izra'eel (عِزْرَاۤئِيْلُ)

4. Q. Are there any other Angels besides those enumerated?

a. Yes, there are many other Angels, some of whom mentioned in the Qur'an are known to us, but we have no knowledge about the number, names and duties of others, which are known only to Allah.

5. Q. What do you know about Angel Jibreel?

A. Angel **Jibreel** was employed by Allah to convey His Messages to His Chosen Ones on earth, the Apostles and the Prophets, who appeared in all ages and all climes. It was the Angel **Jibreel** who communicated the revelations of Allah to our Prohpet Muhammad (May peace and blessings of Allah be upon him).

6. Q. **Can you name some of the main qualities of Angels?**

A. Yes, the main qualities of Angels are purity, righteousness, truthfulness and obedience to the Will and Commands of Allah.

7. Q. **Can Angels do anything on earth without the express permission of Allah?**

A. No, the Angels only act in obedience to the Commands of Allah; hence they cannot do anything on earth without His order.

8. Q. **Do you worship Angels?**

A. No, I do not worship the Angels at all. I adore and pray Allah alone. Angels are the servants of Allah and they too worship Him. The Holy Qur'an explicitly says that we should neither worship anyone but Allah nor should we associate any partner with Him.

CHAPTER III

THE BOOKS OF ALLAH

1. Q. What do you mean by belief in all the Books of Allah?

A. By belief in all the Books of Allah I mean that Allah revealed Commandments and Codes of Religion to various Prophets at different stages of history for the guidance of mankind.

2. Q. **Do you know the names of Codes of Religion or the Books of Allah?**

A. Yes, the Codes of Religion or the Books of Allah are four in number, viz.,

(1) **Taurat** (Old Testament)

(2) **Zaboor** (Psalms)

(3) **Injeel** (New Testament)

(4) The Holy Qur'an.

3. Q. **What are the names of the respective Prophets to whom these books are revealed?**

A. **Taurat** was revealed to Prophet **Moosa** (Moses), Zaboor to Prophet **Dawood** (David), **Injeel** to Prophet 'Isa (Jesus), and the Holy **Qur'an** to Prophet **Muhammad** (May peace and blessings of Allah be upon them all!)

4. Q. **Do the Taurat, Zaboor and Injeel exist in their original forms?**

A. No, they do not exist in their original forms. The present-day editions are only interpretations by their respective followers of later ages.

5. Q. **Which Code of Religion do you follow?**

A. I follow the last Code of Religion, the Holy Qur'an.

14

6. Q. **What is the Holy Qur'an?**

A. The Holy **Qur'an** is the Gospel of the Religion of Islam. The previous Commandments and the Codes of Religion are also incorporated in it. Its verses are inspired and revealed by Allah to Prophet Muhammad through Angel **Jibreel,** and they are still preserved intact in their original form in the Arabic language.

7. Q. **Were the verses of the Holy Qur'an revealed to Prophet Muhammad at one and the same time?**

A. No, the verses of the Holy Qur'an were not revealed to Prophet Muhammad at one and the same time. They were revealed to him either singly or in batches during the last twenty-three years of his life, and were written down at his dictation and arranged under his direction during his lifetime.

8. Q. **What does the Holy Qur'an teach you?**

A. The Holy Qur'an teaches me to worship Almighty Allah, Him and Him alone, to obey His orders contained therein, to follow the teachings and examples set by Prophet Muhammad, to do good to others, especially to my parents and relations, and to be honest and truthful in all my actions and dealings; in short, it gives me a complete Code for the rightful guidance of my life.

CHAPTER IV

THE PROPHETS OF ALLAH

1. Q. What do you mean by belief in all the Prophets of Allah?

A. By belief in all the Prophets of Allah I mean that at different stages of the History of Mankind, Allah sent Prophets as His Messengers for the guidance of mankind. I believe in all of them in general, and in those whose names are mentioned in the Holy Qur'an in particular. I cannot personify anyone as a Prophet if his name is not so mentioned in the Divine Book, nor can I deny the prophethood of any one whose name is so mentioned in the Divine Book.

2. Q. Do you know the names of all the Prophets who delivered the Message of Allah to mankind?

A. No, I do not know the names of all the Prophets who delivered the Message of Allah to mankind, but the names of some of the great Prophets are mentioned in the Holy Qur'an.

3. Q. Can you give a list of the Prophets whose names are mentioned in the Holy Qur'an?

A. Yes. Among the Prophets whose names are mentioned in the Holy Qur'an are:—

> Adam, Idrees, Noah, Hood, Saleh, Ibrahim (Abraham), Isma'il (Ishmael), Ishaq (Issac), Ya'qoob (Jacob), Yusuf (Joseph), Ayyoob, Shu'aib, Moosa (Moses), Haroon (Aaroon), Loot (Lot), Yoonus (Jonah), Al-Jas'a, Zulkifl, Dawood (David), Sulaiman (Solomon), Ilyas (Elias), Zakaria (Zacharias), Yahya, 'Isa (Jesus) and Muhammad.

4. Q. Who are the most important from among these Prophets?

A. They are:—

Adam, Noah, Ibrahim, Moosa, 'Isa and the last and the greatest of all prophets, Muhammad (May peace and blessings of Allah be upon them all!)

5. Q. Who is a Prophet and what is his duty?

A. A Prophet is a Servant and Messenger of Allah who receives the Divine revelations. He is a model for human beings and teaches and practises the Commands of Allah.

6. Q. Do you worship any of the Prophets?

A. No, I do not worship any of the Prophets, but only love and revere them and consider them as models of conduct for myself as well as humanity at large. The Prophets themselves worshipped Allah and taught us to do the same.

7. Q. Can any of the Prophets be called God?

A. None of the Prophets can be called God, for they were all created by Allah Who is Self-Existing and has no partner.

8. Q. Did any of the Prophets claim Divinity?

A. None of the Prophets claimed Divinity, for, besides being Messengers and Servants of Allah, they themselves were human beings.

9. Q. To what land and to what nation did Prophet Muhammad proclaim the Message of Allah?

A. As all the nations of the world had either lost or forgotten the Messages delivered by the Prophets sent to them, Prophet Muhammad proclaimed the Message of Allah to all lands and to all nations. His prophethood is, therefore, not confined to any one land or one nation, but is universal, i.e., for the whole world and for all the nations.

10. Q. Is there any need of a Prophet after Prophet Muhammad?

A. No, there is no need of a Prophet after Prophet Muhammad, for the Message, i.e., the Holy Qur'an (that he has brought for the whole world) is the final and the completest Code of Religion, and is and will be preserved for all time absolutely intact in its original form; besides the authentic record of the Prophet's eventful life covering all human activities is also extant, and will always remain as a Model for mankind. Hence no Prophet either with code and commandments, or without, is required after him, and therefore the Holy Qur'an says that Prophet Muhammad is the last and the Seal of all Prophets.

CHAPTER V

THE DAY OF RESURRECTION AND JUDGMENT

1. Q. What do you know about the Day of Resurrection and Judgment?

A. It is the Day on which Allah will resurrect the dead, i.e., make the dead live again. He will then judge each person according to his good or bad actions on earth. He will reward those who have led a righteous life and pleased Him, by sending them to Heaven, and punish those who have disobeyed His Commands and incurred His displeasure by committing sins and bad actions, by consigning them to Hell.

2. Q. What are Heaven and Hell?

A. Heaven is an abode of peace and happiness where

every wish is fulfilled. Hell is a place of torture, pain and agony.

3. Q. How long will a person remain in Heaven or Hell?

A. A person who dies with complete Faith in the Oneness of Allah and in the Prophet of Allah will remain in Heaven for ever, while a person who dies without having any belief in the Oneness of Allah and in the Prophets of Allah or having belief in others as partners of Allah will remain in Hell for ever.

4. Q. What will be the fate of those who die with complete Faith in the Oneness of Allah and in the Prophets of Allah, but have committed sins?

A. Those who have firm belief in the Oneness of Allah and in the Prophets of Allah, but die without atoning for and repenting sins they have committed in this world, will be sent to Hell for a time, from where, after receiving due punishment, they will be liberated by the Mercy of Allah and sent to Heaven, where they will live for ever.

CHAPTER VI

THE POWER OF DOING GOOD OR EVIL

1. Q. What do you understand by your belief in the power of doing good or evil proceeding form Allah and Allah alone?

A. I mean that Allah has given me the power of action (good or bad), but He has also given me reason and a code of life to choose between good and evil, and therefore, I am responsible for my actions. For example, Allah has given me the power of speaking. It is for me to use the tongue for speaking the truth or abuse its power by speaking lies.

2. Q. How does Allah help you to do good acts?

A. Allah helps us to do good acts by sending Messengers to guide us all along the right path, and Codes of Religion.

3. Q. What is a sin?

A. Any action against the Commands of Allah is a sin.

4. Q. Who can forgive sins?

A. Allah and Allah alone can forgive sins.

5. Q. What should you do, so that Allah may forgive your sins?

A. In order that my sins be forgiven, I must pray to Allah with all my heart and, atoning for all my evil deeds, resolve never to commit any such or other misdeeds again.

6. Q. Which articles of food and drink have been decreed unlawful for a Muslim?

A. The articles of food and drink that have been decreed unlawful for a Muslim are:

(1) All kinds of intoxicating wines, liquors and spirits.

(2) Flesh of swine and all wild animals that employ claws or teeth for killing their victims, e.g., tigers, leopards, elephants, wolves, etc., and all birds of prey as hawks, eagles, vultures, crows, etc.

(3) Rodents, reptiles, worms, etc.,

(4) Flesh of dead animals that are otherwise sanctioned as legitimate.

(5) Flesh of animals and birds (sanctioned) that are not slaughtered or slayed in the prescribed manner.

(6) Flesh of animals that are offered as sacrifice to idols.

7. Q. How should an animal or a bird whose flesh is sanctioned to be lawful for food be slaughtered or slayed?

A. One should say بِسْمِ اللهِ اللهُ اَكْبَرُ "Bismillah" Allahu-Akbar" at the time of slaughtering or slaying an animal or a bird whose flesh is sanctioned to be lawful for food, and pass the knife over its throat in such a manner that the main arteries are cut asunder, but the spinal chord is left alone for a while till all the blood oozes out.

8. Q. Can you name some of the acts that are major sins and are liable for severe punishment

A. Yes. Some of the acts that are major sins and are liable for severe punishment are:—

(1) To believe in anyone as partner of Allah.

(2) To disbelieve in Allah or His Prophets or His Books, or to deny any of the Fundamental Principles of Islam.

(3) To lie.

(4) To committ adultery or sodomy.

(5) To rob or steal.

(6) To cheat or deceive anyone.

(7) To bear false witness.

(8) To bring false charge against anyone.

(9) To backbite.

(10) To abuse anybody or injure anyone's feelings.

PART II

Islam

The Fundamental Principles of Islam

بُنِيَ الْإِسْلَامُ عَلَى خَمْسٍ شَهَادَةِ اَنْ لَّآ اِلٰهَ اِلَّا اللّٰهُ وَاَنَّ
مُحَمَّدًا رَّسُوْلُ اللّٰهِ وَاِقَامِ الصَّلٰوةِ وَاِيْتَاءِ الزَّكٰوةِ وَصَوْمِ
رَمَضَانَ وَحِجِّ الْبَيْتِ مَنِ اسْتَطَاعَ اِلَيْهِ سَبِيْلًا

CHAPTER I

THE DECLARATION OF FAITH

1. Q. **What is the first principle of Islam?**

A. The first principle of Islam is to declare:

La ilaha ill-Allah,
Muhammad-ur-rasool.
ullah.

لَاإِلٰهَ إِلَّا اللّٰه
مُحَمَّدٌ رَسُوْلُ اللّٰه

i.e., "There is no deity but Allah and Muhammad is the Apostle of Allah."

2. Q. **Are there any other forms of the Declaration of Faith?**

A. Yes, there are four other forms, viz.:—

(1) Kalimatush-Shahadat

(كَلِمَةُ الشَّهَادَةِ)

Declaration or Submission of Evidence, viz.,

Ashhadu an la ilaha
ill-Allahu wahdahu
la sharika lahu wa
ashhadu anna Muham-
madan 'abduhu we
rasooluh.

أَشْهَدُ أَنْ لَّاإِلٰهَ إِلَّا اللّٰهُ وَحْدَ
لَاشَرِيْكَ لَهُ وَأَشْهَدُ أَنَّ
مُحَمَّدًا عَبْدُهُ وَرَسُوْلُهُ

i.e., 'I bear witness that there is no deity but Allah, Who is without partner, and I bear witness that Muhammad is His Servant and Apostle.'

(2) Kalimatut-tamjeed

(كَلِمَةُ التَّمْجِيْدِ)

Declaration of the Glory of Allah. viz.,

Subhana-Allahi walhamdu
lillahi wa la ilaha
ill-Allahu wallahu Akbar.
wa la haula wa la quwwata

سُبْحَانَ اللّٰهِ وَالْحَمْدُ لِلّٰهِ وَلَا
إِلٰهَ إِلَّا اللّٰهُ وَاللّٰهُ أَكْبَرُ
وَلَاحَوْلَ وَلَا قُوَّةَ إِلَّا بِاللّٰه

23

illa billahil 'aliyyil-
'Azeem.

الْعَلِيِّ الْعَظِيْمِهْ

i.e., 'Glory be to Allah and praise: there is no deity but Allah; Allah is Most Great; there is no power no might but from Allah the Most High, the Great.

(3) Kalimtut-tauhid   (كَلِمَةُ التَّوْحِيْدِ)

Declaration of the Oneness of Allah: viz.,

La ilaha ill-Allahu   لَا اِلٰهَ اِلَّا اللهُ وَحْدَهُ لَاشَرِيْكَ

wahdahu la sharika

lahu, lahul mulku wa   لَهُ لَهُ الْمُلْكُ وَلَهُ الْحَمْدُ يُحْيِ

lahul hamdu, Yuhyi wa

Yumeetu, biyadihil-   وَيُمِيْتُ بِيَدِهِ الْخَيْرُ وَهُوَعَلٰى

khairu, wa huwa 'ala

kulli shai-in Qadeer.   كُلِّ شَيْءٍ قَدِيْرُهْ

i.e., "There is none worthy of worship but Allah: He is One and has no partner; His is the Kingdom (of the whole universe) and unto Him is due all Praise; He gives life and He causes death: In His hand is all good, and He has power over all things.

(4) Kalimatu raddil-kufr.   (كَلِمَةُ رَدِّ الْكُفْرِ)

Declaration of the
Refutation of Disbelief, viz.,

Allahumma inni a'oozu   اَللّٰهُمَّ اِنِّيْ اَعُوْذُبِكَ مِنْ اَنْ

bika min an ushrika

bika shai'an wa ana   اُشْرِكَ بِكَ شَيْئًا وَّاَنَا اَعْلَمُ

a'lamu wa astaghfiruka

lima la a'lamu innaka   وَاَسْتَغْفِرُكَ لِمَا لَا اَعْلَمُ اِنَّكَ

anta 'Allam ul-ghuyoobi   اَنْتَ عَلَّامُ الْغُيُوْبِ تُبْتُ عَنْهُ وَ

tubtu 'anhu wa tabarr-

r'atu 'an kulli deenin   تَبَرَّأْتُ عَنْ كُلِّ دِيْنٍ سِوٰى دِيْنِ

siwa deen il-Islami wa

24

aslamtu wa aqoolu la
ilaha ill-Allahu Muham-
mad-ur-rasool-ullah.

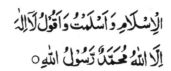

i.t., 'O Allah! verily do I seek refuge in Thee from associating any partner with Thee knowingly; I beseech Thy forgiveness for the sins which I am not aware of; verily, Thou art the Best Knower of all secrets. I repent for all the sins and make myself proof against all teachings except the teachings of Islam. I have entered the fold of Islam, and I hereby declare:— There is no deity but Allah and Muhammad is the Apostle of Allah.

3. Q. Who was Muhammad?

a. Muhammad was the Rasool, i.e., the Messenger and Prophet of Allah who received the Message from Allah through Divine revelation and conveyed the same to humanity.

4. Q. Where was the Prophet Muhammad born?

A. Muhammad, the Messenger and Prophet of Allah, was born at Mecca in Arabia.

5. Q. Do you know the genealogy (Lineage or Pedigree) of the Prophet Muhammad?

A. Yes. I can name up to his father's great-grand-father, and know that he is descended from Prophet Abraham. He was the son of 'Abdullah, who was the son of 'Abdul Muttalib, who was the son of Hashim, who was the sone of 'Abd Manaf.

6. Q. How was the Prophet brought up?

A. 'Abdullah, the Prophet's father died before his birth, and he lost his mother, Amina, during his infancy. He was, then, for a short time under the care of his grand-father, 'Abdul Muttalib, who also expired a few years later. His uncle, Abu Talib, then, became his guardian.

7. Q. How was the Prophet Muhammad (Peace be upon him) educated?

A. He did not receive any instruction through human agency, and as such, he did not know how to read or write. His education was solely due to Divine Sources.

8. Q. When and where was the Message of Allah first received to our Prophet?

A. The Message of Allah was first revealed to our Prophet through angel Jibreel (Gabriel), at the age of forty, in the cave at the foot of Mt. Hira in Mecca.

9. Q. What regard had the people of Mecca for our Prophet before he announced his Prophethood?

A. The people of Mecca had a very great regard for him. They honoured and respected him for his integrity and honesty, and were so much impressed by them and the nobility and gentleness of his character that they conferred upon him the title of اَلْاَمِیْن i.e., the Trustworthy, before he proclaimed his Prophethood.

10. Q. Did the people of Mecca in general accept Muhammad as a Prophet when he first delivered to them the Message from Allah?

A. No. The people of Mecca in general did not accept Muhammad as a Prophet, when he first delivered to them the Message of Allah against idols and idolatry. Only a few embraced Islam. Others persecuted him and his followers so much that he, along with his followers, was compelled to seek refuge in Medina.

11. Q. What is the migration of our Prophet from Mecca to Medina called?

A. The migration of our Prophet from Mecca to Medina is called AL HIJRA. The Muslim Calendar commences from the day of the migration.

12. Q. How did the people of Medina receive our Prophet?

A. Most of the people of Medina received our Prophet with kindness, believed in his teaching and mission and embraced Islam.

13. Q. When did our Prophet die and where was he buried?

A. Our Prophet died at the age of sixty-three and was buried in Medina, where his tomb now stands.

14. Q. Should we visit the tomb of our Prophet?

26

A. Yes, we should visit the tomb of our Prophet at Medina, preferably after the performance of Hajj (Pilgrimage) to Mecca, for our Prophet has said:

مَنْ زَارَ قَبْرِیْ وَجَبَتْ لَهُ شَفَاعَتِیْ

i.e., whoever (of my followers) visits my tomb it is binding on me to plead for (Mercy and Forgiveness) on his (or her) behalf (on the Day of Judgment).

15. Q. **Should you love your Prophet?**

A. Yes, I should love my Prophet and pay greater respect to him than to any other human being including my parents.

CHAPTER II

PRAYER

(اَلصَّلوٰةُ)

1. Q. What is the second Principle of Islam?

A. The second Principle of Islam is to offer the Obligatory Prayers five times a day.

2. Q. What do you understand by Prayer?

A. Prayer is the act of worshipping Allah according to the teaching of the Holy Prophet.

3. Q. What are the essential requisites for offering Prayer?

A. The essential requisites for offering Prayer are:—

(1) The worshipper must be a Muslim.

(2) The worshipper's clothes and body must be free from all impurities.

(3) The place where the Prayer is to be offered should be pure and clean.

(4) The part of the body between the navel and the knees of a male worshipper must be fully covered, and the whole body excepting the hands and face of a female worshipper.

(5) The worshipper must face the Ka'ba in the Great Mosque at Mecca and the direction of Ka'ba outside Mecca.

(6) The worshipper must form the **Niyyat** (i.e., intention) in his or her mind of the particular Prayer, **Fard** (Obligatory) or **Sunnat** or **Nafl (Optional),** he or she is about to offer.

(7) The worshipper must observe the times and rules prescribed for the respective Prayers.

(8) The worshipper must have performed the **Wudu** (i.e., ablution).

(9) The worshipper must have performed **Ghusl** (i.e., the washing of the whole body), if he or she was in a state of grave impurity.

Note:—In order to keep the body clean from dirt and all minor impurities and to be ever ready for prayer, a Muslim must wash the private parts of his or her body with water whenever any impure matter issues from the body.

1. Wudu (ABLUTION) (اَلْوُضُوْءُ)

1. Q. **What is Wudu?**

A. Wudu is the act of washing those parts of the body which are generally exposed.

2. Q. **How do you perform the Wudu?**

A. I perform the **Wudu** in the following manner:—

(1) I make myself sure that the water with which I am going to perform **Wudu** is pure, clean and fresh (not used before) and its colour, taste and smell are unchanged.

(2) I form and have the full intention of performing the **Wudu** for offering prayer.

(3) I recite: "**Bismillahir-Rahmanir-Rahim**" ie., in the Name of Allah, the Beneficent, the Merciful.

(4) I then wash my hands upto the wrists three times, passing the fingers in between each other.

(5) I cleanse my mouth with brush or finger, and gargle with water three times.

(6) Then I rinse the nostrils thrice with water.

(7) I wash the face from the forehead to the chin bone and from ear to ear three times.

(8) I then wash the right arm followed by the left upto the elbows three times.

(9) I then brush up the whole head with wet hands, pass the wet tips of the index finger inside and the wet tips of the thumb outside the ears, and pass over the other surface of the hands over the nape and the sides of the neck.

(10) I then wash the feet upto the ankles, the right foot first and then the left, taking care to wash in between the toes, each three times.

3. Q. What are the Obligatory Acts in the performance of Wudu?

A. The obligatory Acts in the performance of **Wudu** are four, viz:

(1) Washing the face.

(2) Washing both the arms upto the elbows.

(3) Brushing over a quarter of the head with wet hands.

(4) Washing both feet up to the ankles.

Notes:—

(1) If the water to be used for **Wudu** be stagnant, one should make sure that the cistern measures ten yards by ten yards by one foot and is full of water.

(2) If a person wears impermeable foot-gear after the performance of the **Wadu**, it is not necessary to remove it for a fresh **Wadu**. One may just pass over it wet fingers as if one were tracing lines on it. Travellers can take advantage of this concession for three days and three nights, others for one day and one night.

2. GHUSL (BATH) غُسْل

1. Q. When does Ghusl become obligatory?

A. **Ghusl** becomes obligatory after:

(1) Sexual intercourse.

(2) Discharge or effusion of semen.

(3) Completion of menses and confinement.

2. Q. Can you name the obligatory conditions that must be fulfilled for a valid performance of an obligatory Ghusl?

A. The obligatory condition that must be fulfilled for a valid performance of an obligatory **Ghusl** are:

(1) To rinse the mouth thoroughly, so that all the parts are cleaned properly.

(2) To rinse the nose right upto the nasal bone.

(3) To wash all the parts of the body thoroughly, including the hair.

3. Q. **What is the best way of performing an obligatory Ghusl?**

A. The best way of performing in obligatory **Ghusl** is:

(1) The person should have the intention (**Niyyat**) to cleanse the body from grave impurity at the time of performing the bath.

(2) He or she should wash the hands upto the wrists thrice.

(3) Then the private parts must be washed thoroughly thrice.

(4) Filth must be removed, if there be any, from any of the parts of the body.

(5) One should then perform an ablution.

(6) One should lastly wash thrice all the parts of the body, including the hair thoroughly.

3. TAYAMMUM تَيَمُّم

1. Q. **What should a person do in place of Wudu or Ghusl, if one is sick or access cannot be had to water?**

A. When a person is sick or access cannot be had to water, one may perform what is called **Tayammum** in place of **Wudu or Ghusl.**

2. Q. **What are the essential requisites for the performance of a Tayammum?**

A. The essential requisites for the performance of a **Tayammum** are:

(1) To have the intention in mind to perform the **Tayammum** for the removal of impurities.

(2) To strike pure earth lightly with the palms of both the hands.

(3) To pass the palms of the hands over the face once.

(4) To again strike lightly pure earth with the palms of both the hands and rub alternately from the tips of the fingers to the elbows, the forearms and the hands.

3. (a) MISCELLANEOUS NOTES

1. Q. **Do you know the acts or circumstances which make Wudu void?**

31

A. Yes; the acts or circumstances which make the **Wudu** void are:

(1) Answering the call of nature; discharge of semen or issue of worm or sandy stone or any impure matter from the front or the hind private parts.

(2) The passage of wind from the hind private part.

(3) The act of vomitting a mouthful of matter.

(4) Emission of blood, puss or yellow matter from a wound, boil imple., etc., to such an extent that it passes the limits of the mouth of the wound, etc.

(5) Loss of consciousness through sleep, drowsiness, etc.

(6) Temporary insanity, fainting fit, hysteria or intoxication.

(7) Audible laughter during prayer.

2. Q. **Do the same occurences nullify Tayammum also?**

A. Yes; the same occurences nullify **Tayammum** also, but in addition **Tayammum** is nullified as soon as the cause for performing it is removed, i.e., if the sick person recovers, or, if recourse has been taken to it for lack of water, and access to water becomes possible.

3. Q. **What acts are forbidden without the performance of Wudu or the Tayammum as the case may be?**

A. The following three acts are forbidden without the performance of **Wudu** or **Tayammum** as the case may be:

(1) Prayer.

(2) Walking round the Holy Ka'ba in Mecca.

(3) Carrying or touching the Holy Qur'an.

Note:—

Children who have not attained the age of discretion, i.e., about seven years, can carry the Holy Qur'an for the purpose of studying.

4. Q. **Does Wudu convey any inner meaning besides the cleanliness of the body?**

A. Yes, the primary object is cleanliness or purity, but spiritual cleanliness and purity, i.e., freedom from sins which is the main object of religion. It is preferable, therefore, to recite the following after the **Wudu:—**

Allahummaj'alni
minattawwabeena
waj'alni minal
mutatahahhireen.

اَللّٰهُمَّ اجْعَلْنِيْ مِنَ التَّوَّابِيْنَ
وَاجْعَلْنِيْ مِنَ الْمُتَطَهِّرِيْنَ ٥

'O Allah! make me from among those who repent for their sins and from among those who keep themselves pure.

4. AZAN   (اَذَانْ)

1. Q. What is Azan?

A. **Azan** is the first call to Prayer.

2. Q. When and why is the Azan uttered?

A. The **Azan** is uttered in a loud voice to announce to the faithful that it is time for the Obligatory Prayer and to invite them to offer the same.

3. Q. How is Azan recited?

A. **Azan** is recited in a loud voice by the **Muezzin** (the crier) facing the direction of the Ka'ba in the following words which are said in the order mentioned:

(1) Allahu Akbar   (اَللّٰهُ اَكْبَرُ)

i.e., "Allah is Most Great" (four times).

(2) **Ash-hadu an la ilaha ill-Allah.**

(اَشْهَدُ اَنْ لَّا اِلٰهَ اِلَّا اللّٰهُ)

i.e., "I bear witness that there is none worthy of being worshipped except Allah." (twice).

Ash-hadu anna Muhammad-ar-rasoolullah

(اَشْهَدُ اَنَّ مُحَمَّدًا رَّسُوْلُ اللّٰهِ)

i.e., "I bear witness that Muhammad is the Apostle of Allah" (twice).

(4) Hayya 'alas-Salah   (حَیَّ عَلَی الصَّلٰوةِ)

i.e., "Come to Prayer" (turning the face alone to the right and saying it twice).

(5) Hayya 'alal-falah   (حَيَّ عَلَى الْفَلَاحِ)

i.e., "Come to Success" (turning the face alone to the left and saying it twice).

(6) Allahu Akbar   (اَللهُ أَكْبَرُ)

i.e., "Allah is Most Great" (twice).

Ablution and the Prescribed Prayers Illustrated

1. Takbire-Tahrima
Note: The eyes of the worshipper are pinned on the spot where the forehead would rest in Sajdah.

2. QIYAM

3. RUKU
Note: The eyes of the worshipper are pinned
on his toes. He is not to bend too much down
or keep raised up shoulders.

4. QAUMAH

5. SAJDAH
Note: The thumbs of the worshipper are almost in a straight line with the eyes and the fingers all closed together and almost below the ears. The elbows must not touch the floor.

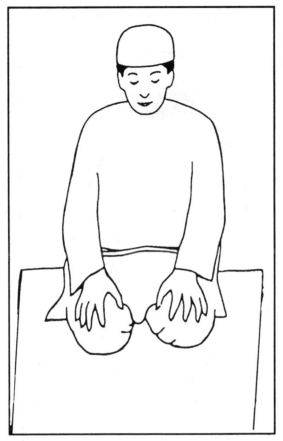

6. JALSA

Note: The eyes are on the lap and the hands rest on the thighs, the fingers not falling on the knees. It is important that one must sit straight fully before resuming the second Sajdah.

7. BACK VIEW OF JALSA AND Q'ADAH

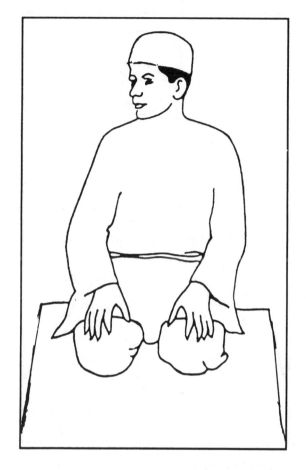

8. RIGHT SALAM
Note: That the eyes of the worshipper are focussed on to his right shoulder.

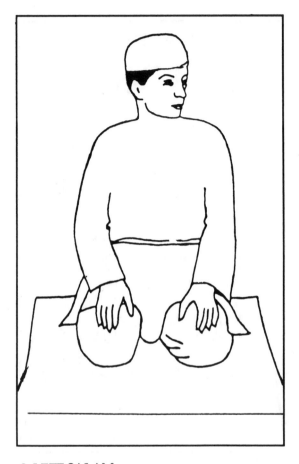

9. LEFT SALAM
Note: That the eyes of the worshipper are focussed on to his left shoulder.

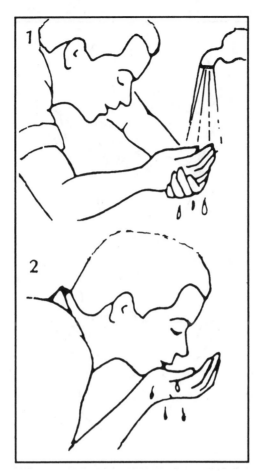

1. Ablution begins with intention (niyyah) that you are making it for the prescribed prayer. You begin by saying, "*Bismillah ir-Rahman ir-Rahim*" (In the Name of Allah, the Beneficent, the Compassionate). Wash both hands up to the wrists three times, making sure that water has reached between your fingers.
2. Put a handful of water into your mouth and rinse it thoroughly three times.

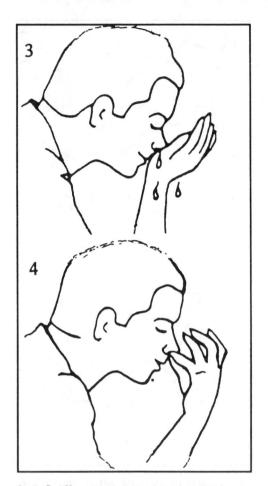

3, 4. Sniff water into your nostrils three times to clean them and then wash the tip of your nose three times.

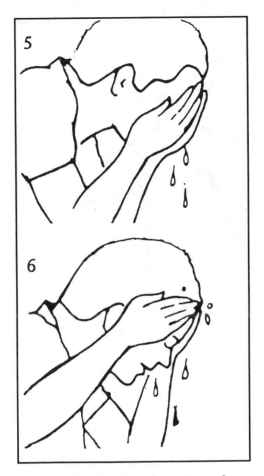

5, 6. Wash your face three times from your right ear to your left ear and from your forehead to your throat.

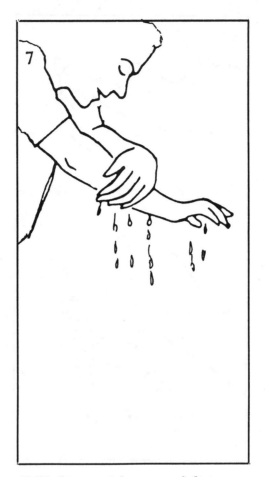

7. Wash your right arm and then your left arm thoroughly from your wrist up to your elbow three times.

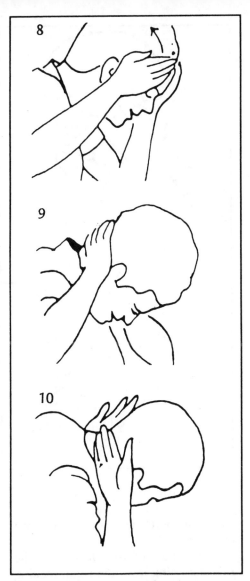

8, 9, 10. Move the inside of your wet hands over your head starting from the top of your forehead to the back and pass your hands over the back of your head to your neck.

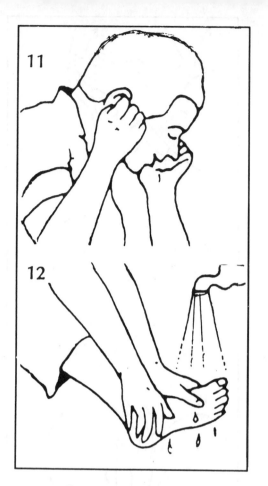

1. Put your wet fingers into the grooves of your ears and ear holes. Also pass your wet thumbs behind your ears.

12. Wash both of your feet up to the ankles starting from the right, making sure that water has reached between your toes and all other parts of your feet. Finish your ablution by reciting: *"Ash-hadu an lā ilāha illal-Lāhu wa ash-hadu anna Muhammadan 'abduhu wa rasūluhu."* (I declare that there is no god but Allah and I also declare that Muhammad is His servant and Messenger.

(7) La ilaha ill-Allah   (الَّا اِلٰهَ اِلَّا اللهُ)

i.e., "There is no deity but Allah (once)."

Note:—The following phrase is added after item (5) in the **Azan** of the early morning prayer, viz., "**As-salatu khairum minannaum**"

(اَلصَّلٰوةُ خَيْرٌ مِّنَ النَّوْمِ)

i.e., "Prayer is better than sleep" (to be said twice).

4. (a) IQAMAT   (اِقَامَةٌ)

1. Q. **What is Iqamat and when is it uttered?**

A. **Iqamat** is the second call to prayer and is uttered immediately before the beginning of the Obligatory Prayer (**fard**). It is similar to **Azan** but with the addition of the sentence, "**Qad qama-tis-Salah**"

قَدْ قَامَتِ الصَّلٰوةُ

i.e., "prayer has indeed begun", to be uttered twice after item (5) above.

5. THE OBLIGATORY AND ESSENTIAL FACTORS OF PRAYER

1. Q. **What are the Obligatory (Fard) Factors in Prayer?**

A. The Obligatory Factors in a Prayer are seven in number:

(1) To say **takbir-i-tahrimah.**

(2) **Qiyam,** i. e., standing erect and placing the right hand upon the left below the navel.

(3) To recite some verses from the Holy Qur'an.

(4) **Ruku',** i.e., bowing down in such a way as to grasp the knees with the hands keeping the back in a straight line so as to form a right angle with the legs.

(5) **Sajdah,** i.e., prostrating in such a way that both the palms of the hands, the forehead, the nasal bone, the knees and the toes of both feet touch the ground; there must be sufficient space between the arms and the chest and the legs and the belly so that they do not touch each other but remain separate.

(6) **Qa'dah,** i.e., sitting down in a reverential posture, keeping the right foot erect on the toes and the left one in a reclining position under the rumps.

(7) To signify the completion of prayer by word or action.

2. Q. Can you name some of the essentials (Wajib) of Prayer?

A. The observance of the following eight points are very essential in any prayer.

(1) To say **takbir-i-tahrima,** viz., "**Allahu-Akbar.**"

(2) To recite the opening chapter of the Holy Qur'an (the **Fatihah**).

(3) To recite any of the other chapters or at least three consecutive verses of the Holy Qur'an.

(4) The recitation of the opening chapter must precede the recitation of any other chapter or three consecutive verses of the Holy Qur'an.

(5) To avoid a pause between the recitation of the opening chapter and any other chapter or three consecutive verses of the Holy Qur'an.

(6) To assume all the postures correctly, *i.e.,* undignified haste must not be practiced in changing the postures·and reasonable pauses must be observed at each stage.

6. PERFORMANCE OF PRAYER

1. Q. **Can you give a complete description of the performance of Prayer?**

A. Yes. A Prayer consists of either two, three or four **Rak'ats,** and a **Rak'at** is perfomed thus:—

(1) I stand erect, facing the direction of Ka'ba in Mecca, and after having the **Niyyat,** i.e., the intention in my mind of what prayer I am about to offer and preferably uttering it to myself;

(2) I raise both of my hands upto the ears and, saying "**Allahu Akbar,**" bring them down and place the right hand upon the left below the navel.

(3) I then recite:—

(a) Subhanak-Alla-
humma wa bihamdika
wa tabarakasmuka wa
ta'ala jadduka wa la
ilaha ghairuka.

سُبْحَانَكَ اللّٰهُمَّ وَبِحَمْدِكَ
وَتَبَارَكَ اسْمُكَ وَتَعَالٰى جَدُّكَ
وَلَا اِلٰهَ غَيْرُكَ ٥

i.e., 'All Glory be to Thee, O Allah! and Praise be to Thee; blessed is
Thy Name and exalted Thy Majesty; and there is none worthy of worship bsides Thee.'

(b) A'oozu billahi
minash-shaitanir-
rajeem.

اَعُوْذُ بِاللّٰهِ مِنَ الشَّيْطَانِ
الرَّجِيْمِ ٥

i.e., 'I betake myself to Allah for refuge from the accursed Satan.'

(c) Bismillah-i-Rah-
man-ir-Raheem.

بِسْمِ اللّٰهِ الرَّحْمٰنِ الرَّحِيْمِ ٥

i.e., (I begin) in the name of Allah, the Beneficent, the Merciful.'

(d) I then recite the Opening Chapter of the **Holy Qur'an (the
Fatiha), viz.,**

Alhamdu lillahi Rabbil-
'aalameen ar-Rahman-
ir-Rahim, Maliki yaum-
-id-deen, iyyakt na'-
budu wa iyyaka nas-
ta'een; ihdinas-sirat-al-
-mustaqeema sirat-alla-
zeena an'amta 'alaihim
ghairil maghdoobi 'alai-
him wal-lad-dalleen.
Ameen!

اَلْحَمْدُ لِلّٰهِ رَبِّ الْعَالَمِيْنَ ٥
الرَّحْمٰنِ الرَّحِيْمِ ٥ مَالِكِ يَوْمِ
الدِّيْنِ ٥ اِيَّاكَ نَعْبُدُ وَاِيَّاكَ
نَسْتَعِيْنُ ٥ اِهْدِنَا الصِّرَاطَ
الْمُسْتَقِيْمَ ٥ صِرَاطَ الَّذِيْنَ اَنْعَمْتَ
عَلَيْهِمْ غَيْرِ الْمَغْضُوْبِ عَلَيْهِمْ
وَلَا الضَّآلِّيْنَ ٥ (اٰمِيْن)

53

i.e., 'All Praise is due to Allah, Lord of the worlds, the Beneficent, the Merciful, Owner of the Day of Judgment. Thee alone we worship and Thee alone we ask for help. Show us the straight path, the path of those whom Thou hast favoured, not (the path of) those who earn Thine anger nor (of) those who go astray. Amen!'

(e) I immediately follow up this by reciting some passage from the Holy Qur'an, which should not consist of less than three consecutive verses. For this purpose any one of the small chapters may be selected, as for instance, the chapter termed "The Unity" viz.:—

Qul huw-Allahu Ahad,

Allahus-Samad, lam

yalid wa lam yoolad,

wa lam yakun lahoo

kufuwan ahad.

قُلْ هُوَاللهُ أَحَدٌ ۝ اَللهُ الصَّمَدُ ۝

لَمْ يَلِدْ وَلَمْ يُوْلَدْ ۝ وَلَمْ يَكُنْ

لَّهُ كُفُوًا أَحَدٌ ۝

i.e., 'Say: He is Allah, the One—Allah, the eternally besought of all! He begets not, nor is He begotten. And there is none comparable unto Him.'

Note:— If a small chapter be recited, it is preferable to precede it by: "**Bismillah-ir-Rahman-ir-Raheem.**"

(f) Then saying "**Allahu Akbar**", I bow down in **Ruku'** and say thrice:—

Subhana Rabbiyal-'Azeem

سُبْحَانَ رَبِّيَ الْعَظِيمِ

i.e., 'How glorious is my Lord, the Great!'

(g) I again assume the standing position, letting the hands remain on the sides and say:

Sami' Allahu liman

hamidah.

Rabbana lakal-hamd.

سَمِعَ اللهُ لِمَنْ حَمِدَهْ

رَبَّنَا لَكَ الْحَمْدُ

i.e., 'Allah has listened to him who has praised him; Our Lord praise be to Thee.'

(h) Then saying "**Allahu Akbar**", I prostrate myself and perform the Sajdah, saying thrice:—

Subhana Rabbiyal-a'la. أَسُبْحَانَ رَبِّيَ الْأَعْلَى

i.e., 'All glory be to my Lord, the Most High.'

(i) I then raise myself and, sitting for a while in a reverential posture, termed **Jalsah**, say once:—

Allahummaghfirli war-
hamni. اَللّٰهُمَّ اغْفِرْ لِيْ وَارْحَمْنِيْ

i.e., 'O Allah! forgive me and have mercy upon me.'

(j) I then perform the second **Sajdah** exactly in the same way as the first one.

This finishes one **Rak'at**. I then say "**Allahu Akbar**", and, standing erect once again, repeat all that I had done in the performance of the first **Rak'at** with the exception of items (a) and (b), which are meant to be recited in the first **Rak'at** only.

(k) After the second **Rak'at's** second **Sajdah** is over, I, saying "**Allahu Akbar**," sit down in the reverential posture called, **Qa'da-tul-Oola** (first sitting) or **Qa'da-tul-Akhira** (last sitting) as the case may be, and recite **Tashahhud** alone in the former case, viz.:—

At-tahiyyatu lillahi was-
salawatu wat-taiyyabatu
assalamu 'alaika ayyu-
hannabiyyu wa rahma-
ullahi wa barakatuhu
assalamu 'alaina wa
'ala 'ibadillah-is-sali-
heen, ash-hadu an la
ilaha ill-Allahu wa ash-
hadu anna Muhamma-
dan 'abduhoo wa
rasooluh.

اَلتَّحِيَّاتُ لِلّٰهِ وَالصَّلَوٰةُ
وَالطَّيِّبَاتُ اَلسَّلَامُ عَلَيْكَ
اَيُّهَا النَّبِيُّ وَرَحْمَةُ اللّٰهِ وَبَرَكَاتُهُ
اَلسَّلَامُ عَلَيْنَا وَعَلٰى عِبَادِاللّٰهِ
الصَّالِحِيْنَ ۚ اَشْهَدُ اَنْ لَّا اِلٰهَ
اِلَّا اللّٰهُ وَاَشْهَدُ اَنَّ مُحَمَّدًا
عَبْدُهٗ وَرَسُوْلُهٗ ۞

i.e., 'All reverence, all worship, all sanctity are due to Allah. Peace be on you O Prophet! and the Mercy of Allah and His Blessings. Peace be on us and all the righteous servants of Allah. I bear witness to the fact that none is deserving of worship except Allah and I bear witness to the fact that Muhammad is His Servant and Apostle.

(1) If more than two Rak'ats are to be performed, I, saying "Allahu Akbar", stand up again, and completing one or two Rak'ats, as the case may be, sit down in the reverential posture called "Qa'datul-Akhira, which is also obviously adopted if the prayer consists of two Rak'ats only. In the reverential posture, I recite in addition to tashahhud, the salawat, viz.,

Allahumma salli 'ala sayyidina Muhammadin wa 'ala ali sayyidina Muhammadin kama sallaita 'ala sayyidina Ibrahima wa 'ala ali sayyidina Ibrahim innaka Hamidun Majeed.

اَللّٰهُمَّ صَلِّ عَلٰى سَيِّدِنَا مُحَمَّدٍ وَّعَلٰى اٰلِ سَيِّدِنَا مُحَمَّدٍ كَمَا صَلَّيْتَ عَلٰى سَيِّدِنَا اِبْرَاهِيْمَ وَعَلٰى اٰلِ سَيِّدِنَا اِبْرَاهِيْمَ اِنَّكَ حَمِيْدٌ مَّجِيْدٌ ٥

Allahumma barik 'ala sayyidina Muhammadin wa 'ala ali sayyidina Muhammadin kama barakta 'ala sayyidina Ibrahima wa 'ala ali sayyidina Ibrahima innaka Hamidun Majeed.

اَللّٰهُمَّ بَارِكْ عَلٰى سَيِّدِنَا مُحَمَّدٍ وَّعَلٰى اٰلِ سَيِّدِنَا مُحَمَّدٍ كَمَا بَارَكْتَ عَلٰى سَيِّدِنَا اِبْرَاهِيْمَ وَعَلٰى اٰلِ سَيِّدِنَا اِبْرَاهِيْمَ اِنَّكَ حَمِيْدٌ مَّجِيْدٌ ٥

i.e., 'O Allah! Shower Thy blessings on our leader Muhammad and his descendants as Thou showeredest Thy blessings on our leader Abraham and his descendants; verily, Thou art the Praise-worthy, the Glorious.

'O Allah! bless our leader Muhammad and his descendents as Thou blessedest our leader Abraham and his descendants; verily, Thou are the Praise-worthy, the Glorious'.

56

(m) I then recite the following du'a:—

Allahumma inni
zalamtu nafsi zulman
kaseeran wa la yagh-
firuz-zunooba illa anta
faghfirli maghfiratan
min'indika war-hamni,
innaka antal-Ghafoor-
ur-Raheem.

اَللّٰهُمَّ اِنِّىْ ظَلَمْتُ نَفْسِىْ ظُلْمًا
كَثِيْرًا وَّ لَا يَغْفِرُ الذُّنُوْبَ اِلَّا
اَنْتَ فَاغْفِرْلِىْ مَغْفِرَةً مِّنْ
عِنْدِكَ وَارْحَمْنِىْ اِنَّكَ اَنْتَ
الْغَفُوْرُ الرَّحِيْمُ ٥

i.e., 'O Allah! I have been extremely unjust to myself and none grants forgiveness against sins but Thou; therefore forgive me Thou with the forgiveness that comes from Thee and have mercy upon me. Verily, Thou art the Forgiver, the Merciful.'

(n) I then turn my face to the right and say the salam:—

اَلسَّلَامُ عَلَيْكُمْ وَرَحْمَةُ اللّٰهِ

Assalamu 'alaikum wa rahmatullah, i.e., 'Peace be upon you and the mercy of Allah'. Then I turn my face to the left and repeat the same.
Here the Prayer is completed.

2. Q. **What should a worshipper do if he or she unconsciously omits any of the essentials of prayer or suspects that he or she has performed more than the prescribed number of ruku's, sajdahs, rak'ats, etc.?**

A. If a worshipper omits any of the essentials of a prayer or suspects that he or she has performed more than the required number of **Ruku's, Sajdahs, Rek'ats**, etc., he or she should perform one **salam** after reciting **Tashahud** and, making two **Sajdahs**, should again recite **Tashahhud, Salawat** and **Du'a** and complete the prayer with the usual two Salams. (This is called **Sajdatus-Sahw**).

3. Q. **What acts nullify a prayer?**

A. The acts that nullify one's prayer are:

(1) Talking.

(2) Doing any three acts in succession.

(3) Emission of impure matter from the body or the annulment of **Wudu** in any way.

(4) Drinking or eating during prayer.

(5) Turning the chest away from the direction of Ka'ba.

(6) Committing breach of any of the obligatory factors of a prayer.

(7) If the body between the navel and the knees becomes uncovered in the case of males, or any part of the body excepting the hands and the face in the case of females.

4. Q. **What does the term Qa'da-tul-Oola mean?**

A. The reverential sitting posture that one adopts after the completion of the two **Rak'ats** of a prayer, consisting of three or four, for reciting **tashahhud** is called **Qa'datul-Oola**.

5. Q. **What is Qa'datul-Akhira?**

A. The final reverential sitting posture which a worshipper assumes after the completion of the prescribed number of **Rak'ats** of any particular prayer, for the recitation of **tashahhud, salawat** and **du'a** is called **Qa'datul Akhira**.

7. CLASSIFICATION OF PRAYERS

1. Q. **How many kinds of Prayers are there?**

A. There are five kinds of Prayers, viz.,

(1) **Fard al-'ain,** i.e., the compulsory prayer that must not be missed on any account whatsoever. This obligatory prayer must be offered at any cost for if one fails to do so he or she will be liable to severe punishment. The nature of its importance is evident from the fact that if one denies its obligatory nature, he or she is classed as an unbeliever.

(2) **Fard al-kifayah** is the kind of prayer which should preferably be offered by all those present at the time, but one at least out of the group must offer it to free the others from responsibility;

for example, if any one individual from amongst the inhabitants of a locality where Death of a Muslim has taken place or from those who join the funeral procession to the cemetery offer the 'Funeral Prayer', the obligation of all concerned is fulfilled.

(3) **Wajib** is a prayer which comes next in rank of **Fard al-'ain** in accordance with the importance attached to it by the Holy Prophet.

(4) **Sunnat-ul-mu'akkadah is the class of prayer which the Holy Prophet used to offer daily without fail and has ordered his followers to do so. One is liable to be questioned for neglecting to offer the same without some very cogent reasons.**

(5) **Sunnatu ghairil-mu'akkadah** is the kind of prayer which the Prophet offered occasionally and desired his followers to do so.

(6) **Nafi** is a voluntary prayer and it is commended for the uplift of one's soul, and for the acquirement of spiritual benefits.

8. FARD PRAYERS

1. Q. **How many kinds of Fard prayers are there?**

A. There are only two kinds of **Fard** prayers, viz.,

(1) The daily obligatory Prayers.

(2) The special congregational Prayers on Fridays.

2. Q. **Can you name the daily Obligatory Prayers?**

A. Yes, the daily Obligatory Prayers are five in number:

(1) **Salatul-Fajr, i.e.,** the early morning prayer which must be offered after dawn and before sunrise.

(2) **Salatus-Zuhr, i.e.,** the early afternoon prayer, the time for which commences immediately after the sun begins to decline, and lasts till it is about midway on its course to setting.

(3) **Salatul-'Asr, i.e.,** the late afternoon prayer which must be offered sometime after the sun is about midway on its course to setting, until a little before it actually begins to set.

(4) **Salatul-Maghrib, i.e.,** the evening prayer which must be offered between the sunset and the disappearance of the light similar to the light at dawn, which follows when the red glow from the horizon in the West has vanished.

(5) **Salatul-'Isha'**, i.e., the night prayer which must be offered any time after the time for **Salatul-Maghrib** comes to an end, and before the break of dawn, but it should preferably be offered before midnight.

3. Q. **How many Rak'ats are compulsory in each of the five daily Obligatory Prayers?**

A. The number of **Rak'ats** compulsory in the five daily Obligatory Prayers are:

(1) Two in **Salatul-Fajr** (the early morning prayer).

(2) Four in **Salatuz-Zuhr** (the afternoon prayer).

(3) Four in **Salatul-'Asr** (the late afternoon prayer).

(4) Three in **Salatul-Maghrib** (the evening prayer).

(5) Four in **Salatul-'Isha'** (the night prayer).

4. Q. **How many Rak'ats of Sunnatul-mu'akkadah should be offered along with each of the five daily Obligatory Prayers?**

A. The number of Rak'ats is as follows:—

(1) Two before the **Fard** of **Salatul-Fajr**.

(2) Four before and two after the **Fard** of **Salatuz-Zuhr**.

(3) None before or after the **Fard** of **Salatul-'Asr**.

(4) Two after the **Fard** of **Salatul-Maghrib**.

(5) Two after the **Fard** of **Salatul-'Isha**.

9. WAJIB-UL-WITR

1. Q. **When is Wajib-ul-witr prayer to be offered?**

A. It should be offered after the **Fard** and **Sunnatul-mu'akkadah** of **Salatul-'Isha.**

2. Q. **Of how many Rak'ats does it consist?**

A. It consists of three **Rak'ats**.

3. Q. **How does it differ from other prayers?**

A. It differs from other prayers in this respect, **viz.**, that, in the third **Rak'at**, before one bows down for the performance of **Ruku'**, one should say: "**Allahu Akbar**", raising the hands unto the ears and after placing them in the former position below the navel, one should recite the following du‘a called **Du‘aal-Qunoot**:—

Allahumma inna nas-
ta‘eenuka wa nastagh-
firuka wa nu'minu bika
wa natawakkalu 'alaika
wa nusni 'alaikal
khaira wa nashkuruka
wa la nakfuruka wa
nakhla‘u wa natruku
manyyafjuruka : Alla-
humma iyyaka
na‘bud. we laka nu-
salli wa nasjudu wa
ilaika nas‘aa wa nah-
fidu wa nargoo rah-
mataka, wa nakhsha
'azabaka inna 'aza-
baka bilkuffari
mulhiq.

اَللّٰهُمَّ اِنَّا نَسْتَعِيْنُكَ وَنَسْتَغْفِرُكَ
وَنُؤْمِنُ بِكَ وَنَتَوَكَّلُ عَلَيْكَ
وَنُثْنِىْ عَلَيْكَ الْخَــيْرَ وَ
نَشْكُرُكَ وَلَا نَكْفُرُكَ وَنَخْـلَعُ
وَنَتْرُكُ مَنْ يَفْجُرُكَ اَللّٰهُـمَّ
اِيَّاكَ نَعْبُدُ وَلَكَ نُصَلِّىْ وَ
نَسْجُدُ وَاِلَيْكَ نَسْعٰى وَنَحْفِدُ
وَنَرْجُوْا رَحْمَتَكَ وَ نَخْشٰى
عَذَابَكَ اِنَّ عَذَابَكَ بِالْكُفَّارِ
مُلْحِقٌ ٥

i.e., 'O Allah! we beseech Thy help and ask Thy pardon and believe in Thee and trust in Thee, and we praise Thee in the best manner and we thank Thee and we are not ungrateful to Thee, and we cast off and foresake one who disobeys Thee. O Allah! Thee alone do we serve and to Thee do we pray and make obeisance and to Thee do we flee and we are quick (in doing so), and we hope for Thy mercy and fear Thy chastisement; surely Thy chastisement overtakes the unbelievers'.

10. SALAT-UL-JANAZAH (FUNERAL PRAYERS)

1. Q. How is Salat-ul-Janazah offered?

A. Salat-ul-Janazah is offered in the congregation as follows:—

(1) The body of the deceased is placed in a coffin and with its face turned towards the ka'ba and the Imam standing by its side with the intention (**Niyyat**) of offering **Salat-ul-Janazah** for that particular dead person raises both hands up to the ears and says "**Allahu Akbar**", the congregation following his lead. The usual **Niyyat** for the **Salat-ul-Janazah** is:

Navaitu an uwaddiya lillahi ta'ala araba'a takbiraati salatiljanazati, ath-thanaau lillahi ta'ala was-salatu lirrasooli wad-du'au lihazal mayyiti (lihazihil mayyiti, in case the deceased is a female), iqtadaitu bihaz al-Imami mutawajjihan ila jihatil Ka'ba-tish-Sharifah.	نَوَيْتُ اَنْ اُوَدِّيَ لِلّٰهِ تَعَالٰى اَرْبَعَ تَكْبِيرَاتِ صَلٰوةِ الْجِنَازَةِ الثَّنَاءُ لِلّٰهِ تَعَالٰى وَ الصَّلٰوةُ لِلرَّسُوْلِ وَ الدُّعَاءِ لِهٰذَا الْمَيِّتِ رَاوُ لِهٰذِهِ الْمَيِّتِ) اِقْتَدَيْتُ بِهٰذَا الْاِمَامِ مُتَوَجِّهًا اِلٰى جِهَةِ الْكَعْبَةِ الشَّرِيْفَةِ ٥

i.e., 'I intend to offer for Allah, the Sublime, four **takbirs** of Funeral Prayer, Praise for Allah, the Sublime, and Blessings (of Allah) for the Apostle and prayer for this deceased person; I adopt the lead of this Imam, with my face turned in the direction of the honoured Ka'ba.'

(2) The Imam and the congregation then join their hands below the navel and recite:—

Subhanak - Allahumma wa bihamdika wa taba-	سُبْحَانَكَ اللّٰهُمَّ وَبِحَمْدِكَ

62

rakasmuka wa ta'ala
jadduka wa jalla tha-
na'uka wa la ilaha
ghairuka.

وَتَبَارَكَ اسْمُكَ وَتَعَالَى جَدُّكَ
وَجَلَّ ثَنَاؤُكَ وَلَا إِلٰهَ غَيْرُكَ

(3) The Imam and the congregation then say **"Allahu Akbar"**, (this time without raising their hands), and recite the salawat as given in (1) item of 3rd part of question (1) in the section on "Performance of Prayer". (See page 56).

(4) The Imam and the congregation then say **"Allahu Akbar"**, as in (2) and recite:—

(a) If the deceased had attained the age of puberty, then the following **Du'a**:—

Allahummaghfir li hay-
yina wa mayyatina wa
shahidina wa gha'ibina
wa saghirina wa kabi-
rina wa zakarina wa
unthana; Allahumma
man ahyaitahu minna
fa-ahyihee 'alal Islam,
wa man tawaffaitahu
minna fatawaffahu 'alal
Iman.

اَللّٰهُمَّ اغْفِرْ لِحَيِّنَا وَمَيِّتِنَا
وَشَاهِدِنَا وَغَائِبِنَا وَصَغِيرِنَا
وَكَبِيرِنَا وَذَكَرِنَا وَأُنْثَانَا
اَللّٰهُمَّ مَنْ أَحْيَيْتَهُ مِنَّا فَأَحْيِهِ
عَلَى الْإِسْلَامِ وَمَنْ تَوَفَّيْتَهُ
مِنَّا فَتَوَفَّهُ عَلَى الْإِيمَانِ

i.e., 'O Allah! Pardon our living and our dead, the present and the absent, the young and the old, the males and the females. O Allah ! (he or she) to whom Thou accordest life, cause him to live in the observation of **Islam**, and he to whom Thou givest death, cause him to die in the state of **Iman**.'

(b) If the deceased is a minor and a boy, then the following **Du'a:**—

Allahummaj'alhu lana
fartan waj'alhu lana
ajran wa zukhran waj-
'alhu lana shafi'an wa
mushaffa'an.

اَللّٰهُمَّ اجْعَلْهُ لَنَا فَرَطًا وَّ
اجْعَلْهُ لَنَآ اَجْرًا وَّ ذُخْرًا
وَّاجْعَلْهُ لَنَا شَافِعًا وَّمُشَفَّعًا

    i.e., 'O Allah! make him our fore-runner, and make him, for us, a reward and a treasure, and make him, for us, a pleader, and accept his pleading.

    (c) If the deceased is a minor and a girl, then the following **Du'a:**—

Allahummaj'alha lana
fartan waj'alha lana
ajran wa zukhran waj-
'alha lana shafi'atan
wa mushaffa'atan.

اَللّٰهُمَّ اجْعَلْهَا لَنَا فَرَطًا وَّ
اجْعَلْهَا لَنَآ اَجْرًا وَّ ذُخْرًا
وَّاجْعَلْهَا لَنَا شَافِعَةً وَّمُشَفَّعَةً

    i.e., 'O Allah! make her our fore-runner, and make her, for us, a reward and a treasure, and make her, for us, a pleader and accept her pleading.'

    (5) Then the Imam and the congregation say "**Allahu Akbar**', as in (3). Then turning their faces alone to the right they say: "**As-salamu 'alaikum wa rahmatullah**". Then they turn their faces (alone) to the left and say: "**Assalamu 'alaikum wa rahmatul-lah**'.

11. THE CURTAILMENT OF OBLIGATORY PRAYERS.

1. Q. When should one curtail the Obligatory Prayer?

    A. When one is travelling with the intention of proceeding forty-eight miles or over from the home, one should offer two **Rak'ats** of Fard Prayers for those which comprise four, and continue to do the same after one's arrival at a destination if one does not intent to prolong his or her stay there for fifteen days or more.

12. FORBIDDEN TIMES FOR PRAYERS

1. Q. **At what time is one prohibited to offer Fard, Sunnat or Nafl prayers?**

A. One is forbidden to offer either **Fard, Sunnat** or **Nafl** prayers at:

(1) The time when the Sun is rising.

(2) The time when the Sun is at its zenith.

(3) The time when the Sun is setting.

2. Q. **Are there any other times when one should not offer the Nafl prayers?**

A. Yes. One should not offer **Nafl** prayers during:—

(1) The interval between the offering of the **Fard** of **Salatul-Fajr** and the rising of the sun.

(2) After the **Iqamat** is called for any congregational prayer at a mosque.

(3) The time between the offering of the **Fard** of **Salatul-'Asr** and the setting of the sun.

(4) The time between the setting of the sun and the offering of the **Fard** of **Maghrib** prayers.

(5) The time between the Imam's getting up from his place for delivering the **Khutba, i.e.,** the sermon, and the completion of Friday congregational Prayers.

(6) At the time of any **Kahutba, e.g.,** Friday, 'Id, etc.

(7) The time between the **Fajr** prayer and the 'Id prayers.

(8) After the 'Id prayers at the premises where the same have been offered.

(9) At the time of **Hajj** in 'Arafat after the **Zuhr** and 'Asr prayers are offered together.

(10) The time between the **Maghrib** and 'Isha prayers at Muzdalifa.

(11) When there is very little time left for offering the **Fards** of any of the daily prayers.

(12) When one feels the need to answer a call of nature.

13. SALAT-UL-JUMU'A (FRIDAY PRAYERS).

1. Q. What is Salat-ul-Jumu'a?

A. It is a congregational Prayer only and cannot be offered alone. Consequently, an Imam (i.e., Leader) is necessary to lead the prayers. The Imam first of all delivers a **Khutba** in two parts consisting of praise to Allah and Prayers of Blessing for the Holy Prophet, and some admonition to the congregation. He then prays to Allah for the welfare of all Muslims. After that he leads two Rak'ats of the Fard of **Jumu'a** and all other follow him, as usual in congregational prayers.

2. Q. Who should be chosen to lead the Prayers?

A. The one most conversant with Islamic theology among those present should be requested to lead the Prayers.

3. Q. How is the Congregational Prayer offered?

A. The Imam stands in front of the congregation facing the direction of the Ka'ba, and all the other worshippers stand in lines behind him and follow his lead, i.e., they stand when he stands, perform **Ruku'** when he does it, and so on.

4. Q. Should a person offering his prayers with a congregation repeat all the requisite recitations?

A. Yes. One should recite everything excepting the Opening Chapter of the Holy Qur'an follow by some other passage from it which the Imam recites on behalf of the congregation.

Notes:—

1. Q. What Prayers are offered in congregation in the daily Prayers?

A. Only the Fard of each Prayer is offered in a congregation, and not **Sunnat** or **Nafl.**

2. Q. What should one do if one misses the congregation for any Prayer (Fard)?

A. If one misses congregation for any Prayer, one should offer it alone or, if possible, join or arrange to have another congregation; but if one misses the congregation of **Salat-ul-Jumu'a** one should offer by oneself the usual **Fard** of **Salat-uz-Zuhr.**

14. WAJIBUL 'ID (THE 'ID PRAYERS).

1. Q. Of how many Rak'ats do the 'Id-ul-Fitr and 'Id-ud-Adha Prayers consist?

A. Each one of them consists of two Rak'ats.

2. Q. How are those two Rak'ats offered?

A. They are offered in the congregation thus:—

(1) The Imam as usual stands in front of the congregation, and facing the direction of the Ka'ba and having the intention of offering the particular prayers says aloud: "**Allahu Akbar**", and the congregation follows his lead.

(2) Then the Imam and the congregation place their hands below the navel as usual, and at short intervals perform three "**takbeers**", i.e., say "Allahu Akbar", raising the hands to the ears and letting them remain at the sides at the end of each "**takbeer**". After the end of third "**takbeer**", the hands are placed below the navel, and the Imam recites **Subhanak Allahumma,** etc.," inaudibly, followed by the audible recitation of **Suratul-Fatiha** (the Opening Chapter) and some other chapter or passage from the Holy Qur'an and finishes the **Rak'at** in the prescribed manner.

(3) In the second **Rak'at,** the order is reversed, for the recitation of Qur'anic passages are made first and **then** the Imam and the congregation perform the three "**takbeers**" as in the first one, and then saying "**Allahu Akbar**" for the fourth time, bow down in the **Ruku'** and complete the prayer as usual.

(4) After the prayer is over, the Imam mounts the pulpit and delivers two **Khutbas** or sermons. At the time of '**Id-ul-Fitr,** the Imam explains the commandments regarding the payment or distribution of **Sadaqat-ul-fitr** and on the occasion of '**Id-ud-Adha,** the commandments about the sacrifice of animals.

Note:—

Q. What are the daily Sunnatu-ghair-il-mu'ak-kadah Prayers?

A. They are:—

(1) Four **Rak'ats** before the **Fard of Salatul-'Asr.**

(2) Four **Rak'ats** before the **Fard of Salatul-'Isha'.**

15. NAFL PRAYERS

1. Q. What are the various special optional (Nafl) Prayers?

A. They are:—

(1) **Salat-ul-Ishraq,** which consists of two or four **Rak'ats** and may be offered after sunrise.

(2) **Salat-ud-Duha,** which consists of two to eight **Rak'ats** and may be offered any time after the **Salat-ul-Ishraq** till the Sun's declination.

(3) **Salat-ul-Tahiyya-tul-Masjid,** which consists of two **Rak'ats** and may be offered on entering a mosque.

(4) **Salat-ul-Tahajjud,** which consists of four to twelve **Rak'ats** and may be offered after mid-night preferably after having slept for some time. This prayer has been specially recommended in the Holy Qur'an for attaining spiritual progress.

(5) **Salatul-Kusufain,** which consists of two **Rak'ats** and may be offered during the eclipse of the Sun or the Moon.

(6) **Salat-ut-Taravih,** which consists of twenty **Rak'ats** and is offered in ten **Salams** of two **Rak'ats** each, each night in the month of Ramadan only after the Obligatory **'Isha** Prayers. It is very commendable to complete the whole Qur'an by reciting consecutive portions of it in each of its **Rak'ats** after the recitation of the **Surat-ul-Fatiha,** and thus finish the whole Qur'an by the end of the month of Ramadan.

16. MISCELLANEOUS

Q. **In which Rak'ats of the prayers is the recitation of the Holy Qur'an made audibly?**

A. The recitation of **Surat-ul-Fatiah** and some other chapter or passage of the Holy Qur'an is made audibly in:

(1) The two **Rak'ats** of the **Fard** of Salatud-Fajr.

(2) The First two **Rak'ats** of the **Fard** of Salatul-Maghrib.

(3) The First two **Rak'ats** of the **Fard** of Salatul-'Isha'.

(4) The two **Rak'ats** of Salatul-Jumu'a.

(5) The two **Rak'ats** of both 'Id Prayers.

(6) In all the twenty **Rak'ats** of the optional **Taraveeh** Prayers in the month of Ramadan.

(7) In the three **Rak'ats** of the **Wajib-ul-Witr** Prayers in the month of Ramadan only.

Q. In what Rak'ats and what Prayers is the recitation of the Holy Qur'an made inaudible?

A. In all the **Rak'ats** of the **Fard** of **Salatuz-Zuhr** and **Salat'Asr** and the last one and two **Rak'ats** respectively of the **Salatul-Maghrib** and the **Salatul-'Isha'**. The **Fatiha** alone is recited in these **Rak'ats** as also in the last two **Rak'ats** of **Salatuz-Zuhr** and **Salatul-'Asr**.

Q. What Prayers should be offered in congregation?

A. The Prayers that should be offered in congregation are:—

(1) All **Fards** of the five Obligatory Prayers.

(2) The **Fard** of **Salatul-Jumu'a**.

(3) Both the **'Id** Prayers.

(4) **Salatut-Taraveeh** in the month of Ramadan.

(5) **Wajib-ul-Witr** in the month of Ramadan only.

(6) Funeral Prayer.

(7) **Salatul-Kausuf**.

CHAPTER III

ZAKAT (Islamic Alms-Fee)

(الزَّكوٰةُ)

1. Q. Can you give the definition of Zakat?

A. Yes. **Zakat** is the amount in kind or coin which a Muslim of means must distribute among the deserving every year.

2. Q. **On whom is Zakat obligatory?**

A. **Zakat** is obligatory on all Muslims who have in their possession for one complete year gold of the minimum weight of seven and a half **tolas** or silver of the minimum weight of fifty-two and a half **tolas** (a tola is equivalent in weight to a Pakistani rupee).

3. Q. **What is the annual rate of Zakat on gold or silver?**

A. The annual rate is 2½%.

4. Q. **Is Zakat obligatory on gold or silver only?**

A. No. It is obligatory not only on gold or silver but also on camels, cattle, goats and all articles of trade.

5. Q. **Is Zakat obligatory on pearls and precious stones?**

A. They are exempted when used as ornaments for personal use, but are liable to **Zakat** as articles of trade.

6. Q. **How should Zakat be calculated on articles of trade?**

A. It should be calculated on the net balance of the value of the articles of trade at the end of the year.

7. Q. **Among what classes of Muslims and for what purposes is the Zakat to be distributed and utilized?**

A. It is distributed among the following classes of Muslims for relieving respective wants:—

(1) The poor Muslims, to relieve distress.

(2) The needy Muslims to supply the implements for earning their livelihood, and those whose hearts are inclined to embrace Islam, i.e., the converts to Islam, the new Muslims to enable them to settle down and meet their sudden needs.

(3) The Muslims in debt, to free them from their liabilities incurred under pressing necessities.

(4) The Muslim wayfarers, if any one of them be found to be stranded in a land foreign or strange to him and stands in need of help.

(5) Muslim prisoners of war, for liberating them by payment of ransom money.

(6) Muslim employees appointed by a Muslim **Amir** for the collection of **Zakat,** for the payment of their wages.

(7) Those engaged in the way of **Allah,** to defray the expenses for the defence and propagation of Islam.

8. Q. **What conditions must be complied with for the fulfillment of the obligation of Zakat?**

A. **Zakat** must be distributed among the classes of Muslims for the purposes enumerated with the **Niyyat** of fulfilling the obligation of **Zakat** and to see to it that the recipient is made the absolute owner in his or her sole right of what is given to him or her.

9. Q. **What moral does Zakat convey to you?**

A. The moral that this institution conveys to me is that I must not be selfish and get too fond of worldly possessions, but must always be ready and willing to help my brethren by all means at my disposal.

SADAQAT-UL-FITR

1. **What is Sadaqat-ul-Fitr?**

A. It is a charity, the annual distribution of which is essential **(Wajib)** for every Muslim who possesses on the last day of the month of Ramadan or the day of '**Id-ul-Fitr** goods of the value which makes them liable for **Zakat.** A Muslim has to pay the **Sadaqat-ul-Fitr** for himself or herself and for his or her minor children.

2. Q. **What is the amount of Sadaqat-ul-Fitr?**

A. One hundred and seventy-five and a half **tolas** of wheat or its equivalent value per head is the minimum amount that a Muslim is enjoined to pay.

3. Q. **To whom should Sadaqat-ul-Fitr be given?**

A. Those who merit **Zakat** also deserve it.

4. Q. **When should Sadaqat-ul-Fitr be distributed?**

A. It should preferably be distributed before offering the '**Id-ul-Fitr** Prayers, otherwise at any other time.

5. Q. **Who are not entitled to receive Zakat or Sadaqat-ul-Fitr?**

They are:

(1) Those on whom payment of **Zakat** is obligatory.

(2) The descendants of the Holy Prophet, however poor they may be.

Note:—

The descendants of the Holy Prophet may accept or be given presents or simple charity, but not **Zakat or Sadaqat-ul-Fitr.**

CHAPTER IV

THE OBSERVATION OF FASTS IN THE MONTH OF RAMADAN

(صَوْمُ رَمَضَانَ)

1. Q. **What do you mean by observation of fasts?**

A. By observation of Fasts I mean the act of abstaining from eating, drinking, smoking, allowing anything whatsoever to enter into what is understood to be the interior of the body, as also voluntary vomitting, self-pollution, sexual intercourse, etc., from the break of dawn till sunset.

2. Q. **On whom is the observation of fasts obligatory?**

A. The observation of fasts is obligatory on all Muslims excepting the infants, the insane, the invalid.

3. Q. **Who is exempted from observing fasts?**

A. Men and women too old and feeble to bear the hardships of a fast are exempted, but they should feed a poor and needy Muslim to satiation twice a day, or pay the amount of one **Sadaqa-ul-Fitr** for every day.

4. Q. **Under what circumstances can one defer the observation of fasts?**

A. One can defer the observation of fasts if:

(1) One is so sick that the observation of fast is likely to increase his or her sickness.

(2) A woman who is suckling a child,and there is a danger of reduction in the supply of milk if she observes fasts.

(3) A traveller who has reason to fear that observing of fasts will make him or her unable to prosecute the journey.

Note:—As soon as one is relieved of the respective disabilities, one must observe the fasts immediately.

5. Q. **Under what circumstances should a woman postpone the observation of fasts?**

A. A woman should postpone the observation of fasts during the period of menses and when she is in the family way.

6. Q. **Why is the observation of fasts obligatory during the month of Ramadan?**

A. The observation of fasts is obligatory in the month of Ramadan because it is the blessed month of the year during which Holy Qur'an was revealed.

7. Q. **Can we spread out the period of fasting and complete the observation of fasts for the required number of days—29 or 30, as the case may be—at any time during the year?**

A. No. The Holy Qur'an enjoins upon Muslims to observe the fasts consecutively for 29 or 30 days, as the case may be, during the month of Ramadan alone. Besides, the main purpose for which the observation of fasts has been made obligatory will not be served if the period were spread out, for the training that one receives for bearing with thirst and hunger, and incidentally realizing the distress of the starving poor and sympathizing with and helping them would not be acquired.

8. Q. **What is the real significance of fasting?**

A. The real significance of fasting consists in the habit of self-control that it fosters and develops and thus enables one to save oneself from being an easy victim to temptation, and consequently minimizing the chances of committing sins. This in its turn will make the practice of virtue easier and lead one nearer to the Kingdom of Allah.

9. Q. What should be done if one does not observe a fast without any cogent reason on any day during the month of Ramadan?

A. If one does not fast on any day during the month of Ramadan without any cogent reason, one will be committing a sin, but all the same he or she must fast on some other day to make amends for the omission.

10. Q. What are the main obligatory factors for the proper observation of fasts?

A. The main obligatory factors for the proper observation of fasts are:

(1) Conception or utterance of **Niyyat, i.e.,** intention to fast.

(2) Abstinence from all things that would nullify the fast from the break of dawn to sunset.

11. Q. What is the usual form of Niyyat for fasting during the month of Ramadan?

A. The usual form of **Niyyat** for fasting during the month of Ramadan is:

Nawaitu sauma ghadin	نَوَيْتُ صَـوْمَ غَدٍ عَنْ أَدَآءِ
'an ada'i fardi Rama-	فَرْضِ رَمَضَانَ هٰذِهِ السَّنَةِ
dana hazihis-sanati	لِلّٰهِ تَعَالٰى
lillahi ta'ala.	

i.e., 'I intend to fast for this day in order to perform my duty towards Allah in the month of Ramadan of the present year'.

12. Q. When should one conceive the Niyyat or give utterance to it?

A. The **Niyyat,** (i.e., the intention) should be conceived or given utterance to for each day preferably before the break of dawn, if not, at any time before midday, if in the meanwhile one has maintained the state of fasting from the time of dawn.

13. Q. What are the main optional (سُنَّةُ) **for the observation of fast?**

74

A. The main optionals for the observation of fasts are:

(1) Partaking of meals before the break of dawn.

(2) Eating of three dates and drinking of water after sunset for signifying the end of the fast.

(3) And reciting, prior to breaking the fast, the **du'a:**—

Allahumma laka sumtu

اَللّٰهُمَّ لَكَ صُمْتُ وَ

wa 'ala rizqika aftartu.

عَلٰى رِزْقِكَ اَفْطَرْتُ

i.e., 'Oh Allah! for Thy sake have I fasted, and (now) I break the fast with the food that comes from Thee!

14. Q. **What is the penalty for doing anything without any cogent reason that makes a fast void?**

A. The penalty for doing anything that makes a fast void without any cogent reason is to observe sixty consecutive fasts or feed sixty persons besides observing the fast in place of one which he or she has deliberately made void.

15. Q. **Is fast made void if by mistake one does something that makes it so under the impression that one is not observing a fast?**

A. No. If anyone by mistake does something that makes a fast void under the impression that one is not observing a fast, the fast is not nullified, provided one stops doing it the moment one recollects the same.

CHAPTER V

PILGRIMAGE TO MECCA

(الْحَجُّ)

1. Q. **On Whom is the performance of Hajj (Pilgrimage to Mecca) incumbent?**

A. The performance of **Hajj** is incumbent on all Muslims, at least once in a life-time, if circumstances permit, i.e., if they are in a position both physically and materially to undertake the journey to Mecca, and make sufficient provision for their dependents during the period of their absence.

2. Q. **How do you define Hajj?**

A. The Pilgrimage to Mecca in the state of **Ihram** to be adopted at the **Miqat** strictly carrying out all that it imposes, observing **wuqoof** at 'Arafat, performing the **tawaf** at Ka'ba, etc., in accordance with the prescribed laws is called **Hajj**.

3. Q. **What is 'Umra?**

A. The visit to Mecca at any time of the year in the state of **Ihram** to be adopted at **Miqat**, performing the **tawaf round** Ka'ba in Mecca and accomplishing sa'ee in accordance with the prescribed laws is called '**Umra.**

4. Q. **What do you mean by Ihram?**

A. The removal of sewn clothes from the body and wrapping it up in a couple of seamless sheets at the **Miqat** with the intention of performing **Hajj** or '**Umra,** and abstaining from all things that are unlawful for those intending to perform **Hajj** or '**Umra** signifies **Ihram.**

5. Q. **What do you understand by Tawaf?**

A. The performance of seven circuits round the Ka'ba (in Mecca) commencing from the Black Stone and having the Ka'ba on one's left is called **Tawaf.**

6. Q. **What does the term Sa'ee signify?**

A. Sa'ee signifies the act of marching to and from between the two hills of Safa and Marwa (near Ka'ba) in accordance with the prescribed laws.

7. Q. **What is Wuqoof?**

A. The stay at 'Arafat, at least for a few minutes, during the time between the declining of the sun from the meridian on the 9th of Zilhijja (the 12th lunar month) and before the dawn of the 10th of Zilhijja is called **Wuqoff.**

8. Q. What territory does Haram constitute?

A. The City of Mecca, in which the Ka'ba is situated along with certain defined outlying territory on all its sides, is called **Haram**.

9. Q. What are Miqats?

A. The boundary lines which the pilgrims or those who want to perform 'Umra should not cross without adopting the **Ihram** are called **Miqats**.

10. Q. How many Miqats are there? What are their names and for whom do they indicate the boundary line of Haram?

A. There are five **Miqats** in all, viz:—

(1) Zul-Hulaifa or Bi'r 'Ali, which indicates the border line of **Haram** for those coming from the side of Medina.

(2) Zat-al-Iraq serves as **Miqat** for those coming from the side of Iraq or Mesopotamia.

(3) Jahfa or Rabigh is the **Miqat** for those from Syria.

(4) Quarn for those from the side of Nedjd.

(5) Yalamlam for those from the direction of Yemen, Pakistan, India, etc.

11. Q. How should a male pilgrim adopt the Ihram?

A. When a male pilgrim is about to cross a **Miqat**, he should perform Ghusl, divest himself of sewn clothes, and wrap up the lower portion of his body in a seamless sheet and cover up the upper part with another one, keeping the head and face bare. The footgear must be such as to keep the central bones of the outer parts of his feet open. He must then offer two **Rak'ats** of **Nafl**, and lastly, he must form in his mind the **Niyyat** and give utterance to his intention as to the purpose of his adopting the **Ihram**.

12. Q. What is the form of Niyyat for Hajj?

A. The form of **Niyyat** for the Hajj is:—

Allahumma inni uri-
dulhajja fayyassirhu li
wa taqabbalhu minni,

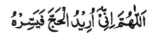

nawaitul-hajja wa ah-
ramtu bihi mukhlisan
lillahi ta'ala.

إِلِي وَتَقَبَّلَهُ مِنِّي نَوَيْتُ الْحَجَّ وَأَحْرَمْتُ بِهِ مُخْلِصًا لِلَّهِ تَعَالَى

i.e., 'O Allah! I intend to perform the Hajj. Make Thou the same easy for me and accept it from me. I have conceived the Niyyat for Hajj and I have adopted the Ihram sincerely for Allah, the Sublime.'

13. Q. What is the form of Niyyat for 'Umra?

A. If one wants to perform only 'Urma he or she should say:

Allahumma inni uridul
'Umrata fayassirha li
wa taqabbalha minni,
nawaitul-'Umrata wa
ahramtu biha mukh-
lisan lillahi ta'ala.

اَللّٰهُمَّ إِنِّيٓ أُرِيدُ الْعُمْرَةَ فَيَسِّرْهَالِيْ وَتَقَبَّلْهَا مِنِّي نَوَيْتُ الْعُمْرَةَ وَأَحْرَمْتُ بِهَا مُخْلِصًا لِلَّهِ تَعَالَى

i.e., 'O Allah! I intend to perform 'Umra. Make Thou the same easy for me and accept it from me. I have conceived the 'intention' for 'Umra and have adopted the Ihram for it, sincerely for the sake of Allah, the Sublime.'

14. Q. What is the form of Niyyat for performing Hajj and 'Umra together?

A. It is:—

Allahumma inni uri-
dulhajja wal 'Umrata
fayassirhuma li wa ta-
qabbalhuma minni, na-
waitul Hajja wal 'Um-
rata wa ahramtu bi-
hima mukhlisan lillahi
ta'ala.

اَللّٰهُمَّ إِنِّيٓ أُرِيدُ الْحَجَّ وَ الْعُمْرَةَ فَيَسِّرْهُمَالِيْ وَ تَقَبَّلْهُمَا مِنِّي نَوَيْتُ الْحَجَّ وَالْعُمْرَةَ وَأَحْرَمْتُ بِهِمَا مُخْلِصًا لِلَّهِ تَعَالَى

i.e., 'O Allah! I intend to perform both **Hajj** and **'Umra.** Make Thou the same easy for me and accept them from me. I have conceived the intention for both **Hajj** and **'Umra** and have adopted the **Ihram** to perform both **Hajj** and **'Umra** only for the sake of Allah, the Sublime.'

15. Q. **What should one do after one has given utterance to one of the appropriate Niyyats?**

A. After one has given utterance to one of the **Niyyats,** one should say aloud (these words should be perfectly committed to memory as one will have to recite them again and again, sitting, standing, mounting and dismounting):

Labbaik Allahumma
labbaik; labbaika la
sharika laka labbaik;
innal-hamda wan ni'-
mata laka wal mulka
la sharika lak.

لَبَّيْكَ ٱللّٰهُمَّ لَبَّيْكَ لَبَّيْكَ
لَا شَرِيكَ لَكَ لَبَّيْكَ إِنَّ
الْحَمْدَ وَالنِّعْمَةَ لَكَ وَالْمُلْكَ
لَا شَرِيكَ لَكَ

i.e., 'Here I am at Thy service. O Allah! Here I am at Thy service; Here I am at Thy service; There is no partner unto Thee; Here I am at Thy service; To Thee the glory, the riches and the sovereignty of the world. There is no partner to Thee.'

16. Q. **What things become unlawful for those adopting the Ihram?**

A. The things that become unlawful for those adopting the **Ihram** and remain as such till the object for which the **Ihram** has been adopted is accomplished are:

(1) Hunting or aiding and abetting it.

(2) Sexual intercourse or its preliminaries.

(3) Cropping or shaving of hair or paring of nails.

(4) Covering of head or face in any way whatsoever.

(5) Use of gloves or socks.

(6) Wearing of any kinds of sewn clothes or underwear.

(7) Using any perfume or perfumed preparation.

(8). Deliberate smelling of perfume or applying it to any part of the body or the sheets covering it, or even keeping it in any manner on one's person. (If any aroma of perfumes applied before the conception of **Niyyat** remains, it does not matter, for it is permissible).

(9) Killing or even dislodging and throwing away lice if they happen to find their way on one's person or the sheets covering it.

17. Q. What is the difference between the adoption of Ihram by men and women?

A. The points of difference between the adoption of Ihram by men and women are:

(1) That a woman can wear sewn clothes.

(2) She can cover her head (as a matter of fact she should cover her head in the presence of all men excepting her husband, as also whilst offering prayers).

(3). She should not put on a veil in such a manner that the fabric may touch her face.

(4) She can put on socks or gloves.

(5) All the other things which are unlawful for a man are also unlawful for her.

Note:—A woman should not utter "**labbaik**", etc., aloud but should say the same in a subdued voice.

18. Q.   How is the Tawaf performed?

A. The points to be observed in the performance of **Tawaf** are:

(1) The performer of **Tawaf** should stand towards that corner of the Ka'ba where the black stone is embedded in its wall in such a manner as to have it on one's right and then give utterance to the **Niyyat** or performing it in the words:

Allahumma inni uridu
tawafa baitikalmuhar-
rami fayassirhu li wa
taqabbalhu minni.

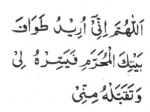

i.e., 'O Allah! I intend to perform the **tawaf** of Thy consecrated premises. Make Thou the same easy for me and accept it from me'.

(2) Then facing the Black Stone and raising the hands with palm outwards, one should say:

Bismillahi walhamdu
lillahi wallahu Akbar
wassalatu was-salamu
'ala Rasoolillah.

بِسْمِ اللهِ وَالْحَمْدُ لِلهِ وَ
اللهُ أَكْبَرُ وَالصَّلوةُ وَالسَّلَامُ
عَلَى رَسُولِ اللهِ

i.e., "I begin in the name of Allah, and all Praise is due to Allah and Allah is Most Great, and peace and blessings be on Allah's Apostle."

(3) If possible one should approach the Black Stone and give it a kiss, but if it be not feasible, then one should give it a flying kiss, and recite the **Du'a**:—

(a) Allahummaghfirli
zunoobi wa tahhir li
qalbi wa ashrah li sadri
wa yassir li amri wa
'afini fi man 'afait.

اَللّٰهُمَّ اغْفِرْ لِي ذُنُوبِي وَ
طَهِّرْ لِي قَلْبِي وَاشْرَحْ لِي
صَدْرِي وَيَسِّرْ لِي أَمْرِي وَ
عَافِنِي فِيمَنْ عَافَيْتَ

i.e., 'O Allah! forgive me my sins and purify my heart and expand my chest (i.e., give me spiritual illumination) and make my task easy and preserve me among those Thou hast preserved.'

(b) Then one should proceed towards the Gate of Ka'ba saying:—

Allahumma imanam
bika wa tasdiqan bi-
kitabika wa wafa'an bi-
'ahdika wattiba'an li
sunnati nabiyyika Mu-
hammadun, sallallahu

اَللّٰهُمَّ إِيمَانًا بِكَ وَتَصْدِيقًا
بِكِتَابِكَ وَوَفَاءً بِعَهْدِكَ وَ
اتِّبَاعًا لِسُنَّةِ نَبِيِّكَ مُحَمَّدٌ
صَلَّى اللهُ تَعَالَى عَلَيْهِ وَسَلَّمَ

81

ta'ala 'alaihi wa sal-
lama, wa ashhadu an la
ilaha ill-Allahu wahda-
hu la sharika lahu wa
ashhadu anna Muham-
madan 'abduhu wa
rasooluhu, amantu bil-
lahi wa kafartu bil-jibti
wattaghoot.

وَ اَشْهَدُ اَنْ لَّا إِلٰهَ إِلَّا اللهُ
وَحْدَهُ لَا شَرِيْكَ لَهُ وَاَشْهَدُ
اَنَّ مُحَمَّدًا عَبْدُهُ وَ رَسُوْلُهُ
اٰمَنْتُ بِاللهِ وَ كَفَرْتُ
بِالْجِبْتِ وَالطَّاغُوْتِ

i.e., 'Oh Allah! (I am performing this) with complete Faith in Thee
and Belief in the Truth of Thy Book and in the fulfilment of my pledge
to Thee, and in the wake of the **sunnat** of Thy Prophet Muhammad, may
peace and blessing of Allah be upon him. I bear witness to the fact that
there is no God but Allah and that Muhammad is His Prophet. I have
faith in Allah and do not believe in evil spirits and ghosts.

Note:—The act of kissing the Black Stone and reciting **du'a** is called
Istilam.

(4) Then, having the Ka'ba on one's left, one should take a complete round of it, remembering Allah all the while or reciting
Du'a (a and b of 3) in the same way as before. This completes
one circuit.

Note:—One may kiss, if possible the South-West corner of Ka'ba which
is called **Rukn-i Yamani.**

(5) One should perform seven rounds in the manner described.

(6) After the completion of seven rounds one should stand near the
gate of Ka'ba and pray for Allah's blessings.

(7) Lastly, one should offer two Rak'ats of Sunnatut-tawaf, preferably near Maqam-i-Ibrahim, a spot just near the Ka'ba.

19. Q. **What acts are culpable during the performance of
tawaf?**

A. The acts that are culpable during the performance of **tawaf**
are:

(1) Being without ablution.

(2) Uncovering of more than a quarter part of any limb of the body which must be kept covered.

(3) Performing of the tawaf either by supporting oneself on someone's shoulder or mounted, without any cogent reason.

(4) Performing the tawaf in a sitting posture without any cogent reason.

(5) Performing the tawaf with the Ka'ba on one's right.

(6) Performing the tawaf round The Ka'ba exclusive of Hatim (Hatim is the name for the portion of land in the North of Ka'ba which was left out when the Ka'ba was rebuilt).

(7) Performing a lesser number of circuits than seven.

20. Q. **What acts are not permissible during the performance of Tawaf?**

A. Such acts are:—

(1) Discussion of mundane matters.

(2) The performance of Tawaf in an impure garb.

(3) The disregard of Ramal which signifies marching briskly, moving the shoulders with chest out, like the gait of a soldier, in the first three circuits of the Tawaf of 'Umra.

(4) The disregard of Iztiba'a, which denotes the act of removing the sheet from the right shoulder and passing it under the right armpit to place it on the left shoulder, thus keeping bare the right arm in the Tawaf of 'Umra.

(5) Omission of Istilam.

(6) Pauses between the cirucits of Tawaf (Of course if the Wudu is made void or a congregation of an Obligatory Prayer is ready, one may discontinue the circuits to perform the Wudu or to join the congregation and complete them later on).

(7) The failure to offer two Rak'ats of Nafl after the completion of each Tawaf, i.e., seven circuits of the Ka'ba (if the time be, however, one when it is not permissible to offer the prayers, one is allowed to defer the same till the completion of the second Tawaf).

SA'EE

21. Q. How should the Sa'ee be performed?

A. In order to perform the Sa'ee one should betake himself to Safa and after arriving there recite:—

(1) Abda'u bima bada'
Allahu bihi, innas-Safa
wal Marwata min sha-
'a-'irillahi, faman hajj-
al-baita awi'tamara
fala junaha 'alaihi any-
yat-tawwafa bihima
wa man tatawwa'a
khairan fa inn-Allah
Shakirun 'Aleem.

ٱبۡدَٲُ بِمَا بَدَٲَ ٱللّٰهُ بِهٖ اِنَّ الصَّفَا وَالۡمَرۡوَةَ مِنۡ شَعَآٮِرِ اللّٰهِ فَمَنۡ حَجَّ الۡبَيۡتَ اَوِاعۡتَمَرَ فَلَاجُنَاحَ عَلَيۡهِ اَنۡ يَّطَّوَّنَ بِهِمَا وَمَنۡ تَطَوَّعَ خَيۡرًا فَاِنَّ اللّٰهَ شَاكِرٌ عَلِيۡمٌ ٥

i.e., 'I commence with that with which Allah commenced. Surely Safa and Marwa are prominent symbols of Allah. Hence there is no blame on one who performs the **Hajj** of the House (of God) or **'Umra** if he (or she) marches to and from between them (Safa and Marwa), and one who does good of one's own accord, verily Allah is Responsive, Aware'.

(2) Then, raising the hands to the shoulders, one must say:

    (a) **Allahu Akbar** (thrice),
    and (b) **La ilaha illallahu wallahu Akbar wa lillahilhamd.**

(3) Then one should give utterance to his or her **Niyyat** in the words:—

Allahumma inni uridus-
Sa'ya bainas-Safa wal
Marwati fayassirhu li
wa taqabbalhu minni.

ٱللّٰهُمَّ اِنِّيۡ اُرِيۡدُ السَّعۡيَ بَيۡنَ الصَّفَا وَالۡمَرۡوَةِ فَيَسِّرۡهُ لِيۡ وَتَقَبَّلۡهُ مِنِّيۡ

i.e., 'O Allah! I intend to perform the **Sa'ee** between Safa and Marwa; make Thou the same easy for me and accept it from me'.

(4) Then one should march towards Marwa, reciting **Du'as** all the way.

(5) When one reaches a green spot one should march quickly till one reaches another green spot, and in between those spots one should recite the following **Du'a:—**

Rabbighfir warham wa tajawaz 'amma ta'lam wa ta'lamu ma la na'- lam innaka antal-A'az- zul-Akram; Allahum- maj'alhu hajjammab- rooran, wa sa'yam- mashkooran, wa zam bammaghfoora.

رَبِّ اغْفِرْ وَارْحَمْ وَ تَجَاوَزْ

عَنْ مَا تَعْلَمُ وَ تَعْلَمُ مَالَا

نَعْلَمُ اِنَّكَ اَنْتَ الْاَعَزُّ الْاَكْرَمُ

اَللّٰهُمَّ اجْعَلْهُ حَجًّا مَبْرُوْرًا

وَّ سَعْيًا مَشْكُوْرًا وَّ ذَنْبًا

مَغْفُوْرًا

i.e., 'O Allah! Forgive me and have mercy upon me and pass off (my sins) of which Thou art aware, and Thou knowest that of which we have no knowledge; verily Thou art the Most Honourable, the Most Exalted. O Allah! make it (for me) a **Hajj** that is acceptable (to Thee) and an effort that is granted and (a means of) forgiveness of sin!

(6) Arriving at Marwa one should face Ka'ba and pray for blessings (this completes one turn).

(7) Then one must go back to Safa in the same manner, marching quickly between the two green spots, reciting **Du'as**, etc., and when Safa is reached one must again face the Ka'ba and pray for blessing (this will complete the second turn).

(8) One must take seven such turns, and at the accomplishment of the seventh, when one arrives at Marwa and offers up the prayer one is said to have accomplished the Sa'ee.

THE PERFORMANCE OF HAJJ

1. Q. **Can you describe the performance of Hajj?**

A. Yes, in order to perform **Hajj**:—

(1) As soon as a pilgrim approaches the boundary line of the Holy Land, i.e., the **Miqat**, he or she enters the state of **Ihram** with all its accompaniments.

(2) On reaching Mecca the pilgrim goes to the Grand Mosque round the Ka'ba and then performs an optional **tawaf**, called **Tawaf-ul-Qudoom**.

(3) On the 8th day of Zilhijja the pilgrim goes to Mina, before the time of **Salatuz-Zuhr**, a town three miles from Mecca, and spends there the rest of the day and the whole night of the 9th Zilhijja.

(4) After the earling morning prayer of the 9th Zilhijja, the pilgrim proceeds to 'Arafat, a place about seven miles from Mecca, and stops anywhere in the **Mauqafs** (staying places) in the area surrounding the **Jabal-i-Rahmat**, (i.e., the Hill of Mercy) in the rememberance of Allah.

(5) Just after the sunset of the 9th Zilhijja the pilgrim leaves the **Mauqaf** without offering **Salatul-Maghrib**, and proceeds to Muzdalifa, a place between Mina and 'Arafat, where he or she offers **Maghrib** and 'Isha prayers.

(6) The pilgrim then proceeds from Muzdalifa after the early morning prayers of the 10th of Zilhijja (picking at least 49 pebbles from there) and comes to Mina.

(7) The pilgrim then takes up seven pebbles, and holding each between the index finger and the thumb of the right hand, throws them one by one at the pillar called **Jamra-tul-'Uqubah** on the same day, i.e., the 10th Zilhijja.

(8) The pilgrim then, if he or she can afford, makes a sacrifice of a goat or a sheep or joins six others in the sacrifice of a camel or a bull, and shaves off preferably the whole head or at least a quarter head, or crop the hair equally all over the head, if the pilgrim be male, and in the case of a female pilgrim, she should cut off at least an inch of her hair.

(9) The pilgrim then leaves off the state of **Ihram** and proceeds to Mecca on the same day and performs the **Tawaf**, called **Tawaf ul-Ifada**, after which the pilgrim offers two **Rak'ats** of **Sunnat** prayers.

(10) The pilgrim then accomplishes the **Sa'ee**.

(11) The pilgrim then returns to Mina and spends there the night of the 11th of Zilhijja.

(12) After the midday of the 11th and the 12th of Zilhijja the pilgrim approaches in the order mentioned, the pillars called **Jamra-tul-Oola, Jamratul-Wusta** and **Jamratul-'Uqubah,** and throws seven pebbles against each of them, reciting at each throw: "**Bismillahi Allahu Akbar.**" If a pilgrim stays on the 13th of Zilhijja as well, he or she throws seven pebbles at the pillars as on the two previous days.

(13) The pilgrim then returns to Mecca after the **Salatuz-Zuhr** on the 12th of Zilhijja. Before leaving Mecca for one's own country, the pilgrim, performs a departing tawaf, called **Tawaf-ul-Wida'.**

Notes:—

(1) During one's stay at Mecca one may perform as many **tawafs** as one can, for the performance of **tawafs** is the best form of worship during that period.

(2) One can also perform 'Umra as many times as one likes by going out of Mecca to Tan'eem (a place about three miles from Mecca) and adopting the **Ihram** there, return to Mecca and perform the **tawaf** and sa'ee as is usual for 'Umra.

2. Q. **How does one perform 'Umra?**

A. In order to perform the 'Urma one should in the first instance:

(1) Adopt the **Ihram** at the **Miqat** in accordance with the prescribed laws.

(2) After proceeding to Mecca one should betake himself or herself to Ka'ba and affecting the **Iztiba'a,** one should form and give utterance to the **Niyyat** for **Tawaf** and commence the performance of the same.

(3) One should take care to perform the first three circuits in the style of **Ramal.**

Note:—A woman is, however, exempt both from **Iztiba'a** and **Ramal.**

(4) After the completion of the three cirucits, the remaining four are performed in the normal manner and one should then offer two **Rak'ats** of **Sunna-tut-Tawaf.**

87

(5) One should then preferably proceed to the well of Zamzam and drink a little water.

(6) From thence, betaking oneself to Safa, one should accomplish the Sa'ee according to the prescribed laws.

Note:—The performance of 'Umra is completed after the accomplishment of the Sa'ee. Now if one wants to perform the Hajj in the very Ihram, one may maintain the same; but if one does not want to do so, one should shave off at least a quarter or preferably the whole head or crop the hair all over the head. The pilgrim is then free from all the impositions and restrictions that the state of Ihram imposes.

3. Q. **Can Hajj and 'Umra be performed in the same state of Ihram?**

A. Yes, **Hajj** and 'Umra can be performed in the same state of **Ihram,** in which case the pilgrim should not leave off the state of **Ihram** after the performance of 'Umra till the completion of **Hajj.**

4. Q. **What is Qiran?**

A. When the **Hajj** and 'Umra is performed in the same state of **Ihram,** it is called **Qiran.**

5. Q. **What is Tamattu?**

A. When the 'Umra is performed in the month of Hajj and then **Ihram** is removed and re-donned on the 7th of Zilhijja at Mecca for the second time for **Hajj,** it is called **Tamattu'.**

Note:—One who performs **Qiran** or **Tamattu'** is bound to sacrifice a goat or sheep or join six others in the sacrifice of a camel or a bull, or observe ten fasts, three before **Hajj** and seven after its performance.

6. Q. **What is Ifrad?**

A. If one performs Hajj alone and not 'Umra, it is called **Ifrad.**

Note:—The sacrifice of an animal is not obligatory on one performing the **Hajj** alone, i.e., **Ifrad.**

(2) If anyone of the essential observances in connection with **Ihram, Tawaf** or **Sa'ee** are transgressed, one is liable for penalties in the shape of either sacrificing a goat or a sheep, or distributing alms. Further particulars in detail will be dealt with in our next volume.

7. Q. What should a pilgrim do after performing Hajj?

A. It is very commendable for a pilgrim to pay a visit to the Mausoleum of the Holy Prophet at Medina, and standing there in a reverential posture facing the tomb of the Great Prophet, to say:—

Assalamu 'alaika ayyu-han-Nabiyyu wa rah-matullahi wa baraka-tuhu, Assalamu 'alaika ya Rasoolallah! Assalamu 'alaika ya Nabi-Allah! Assalamu 'alaika ya Habib Allah Assalamu 'alaika ya khaira-khalqillah! As-salamu 'alaika ya Sha-fi'-al-muznibeen! Assa-lamu 'alaika wa 'ala alika wa as-habika wa ummatika ajma'een

السَّلَامُ عَلَيْكَ أَيُّهَا النَّبِيُّ
وَرَحْمَةُ اللهِ وَبَرَكَاتُهُ
السَّلَامُ عَلَيْكَ يَا رَسُوْلَ اللهِ
السَّلَامُ عَلَيْكَ يَا نَبِيَّ اللهِ
السَّلَامُ عَلَيْكَ يَا حَبِيْبَ اللهِ
السَّلَامُ عَلَيْكَ يَا خَيْرَ خَلْقِ اللهِ
السَّلَامُ عَلَيْكَ يَا شَفِيْعَ
الْمُذْنِبِيْنَ السَّلَامُ عَلَيْكَ وَ
عَلَى آلِكَ وَأَصْحَابِكَ وَأُمَّتِكَ
أَجْمَعِيْنَ

i.e., 'Peace be on you, O Prophet (of Allah)! and His mercy and His blessings. Peace be on you, O Apostle Allah! Peace be on you O Prophet of Allah! Peace be on you, O Beloved of Allah! Peace be on you, O Best in the (whole) Creation of Allah! Peace be on you, O Pleader for the sinners (before Allah)! Peace be on you and your descendants and your companions and all your followers.

——— :o: ———

The End

89

'ID PRAYERS
(SALATUL 'IDAIN)

'ID PRAYERS

(SALATUL 'IDAIN)

'ID PRAYERS (SALATUL 'IDAIN)

'Id prayer is a strongly recommended and important tradition in Islam and the Prophet (peace be upon him) never neglected it. He is reported to have ordered the men, women and children to proceed to the 'Id prayer ground.

Even menstruating women are encouraged to go to the 'Id ground but they should keep away from the actual place of prayer.

SELF PREPARATION FOR 'ID PRAYER

It is highly recommended to have major ablution (Islamically correct bath or *ghusl*) and to use the most beautiful dresses and the best perfumes one can obtain. The Prophet (peace be upon him) used to do so. There is also a tradition that one should eat something, preferably dates, before going to the 'Id ul Fitr prayer and to eat nothing before 'Id ul Adha prayer.

Time:

The time for 'Id ul Adha is when the sun has risen two meters (7 ft.) above the horizon and the time for 'Id ul Fitr is while the sun has risen to three meters (10 ft.) above the horizon. 'Id prayers cannot be said after midday.

Place:

It is better to hold 'Id prayers in an open place or ground if there is no obstacle like rain or bad weather. The Prophet never performed 'Id prayers in the mosque except once due to rain.

No Adhan, No Iqamah:

There is neither *Adhan* nor *Iqama* for 'Id prayers

Performance of 'Id Prayers:

'Id prayer consists of two *Rak'a* with twelve *takbeeras*, (Allahu Akbar), seven in the first *Rak'a* and five in the second. In the first *Rak'a* just

1

after *takbeeratul Ihram*, say seven *Takbeeras* lifting your hands with each *Takbeera* and after finishing seven *Takbeeras* go on with prayer in the usual way (reading al Fatiha and a surah aloud.) In the beginning of the second *Rak'a* say five *Takbeeras* in the usual way. There is no special Dhikr between *Takbeeras* — you can say *Subhanalla Walhamdu Lillahi Wa Laa Ilaha Illallahu Wallahu Akbar.*

Khutba:

After performing the *Salat*, the Imam must deliver a *khutba* just like jum'a khutba. But Imam Nawawi and some other scholars say that the *khutba* of 'Id is not broken up into two parts with a period of sitting in between.

Returning:

On returning home from the *salat*, it is recommended to take a different route than that which was taken to the prayer.

Takbir:

It is strongly recommended to repeat in a loud voice (a) *Allahu Akbar*, on the way to the *salat* and while waiting for the *imam*; (b) to repeat Allahu Akbar, Allahu Akbar, La ilaha illa Allahu, wa Allahu Akbar, wa lillahi-I-hamd after every congregational prayer starting from the fajr, (dawn prayer) on the day of Arafat (ninth day of Zhul Hijja), to the 'asr (afternoon prayer) on the last of the *Days of Tashriq* (the thirteenth day of Dhul Hijja). For the Pilgrims, the starting time is the *dhur*, (noon prayer) of the *Day of Nahr* (tenth of Dhul Hijja).

It is clear that this takbir applies only to 'Id ul Adha while the first applies to both.

Zakatul Fitr:

Zakatul Fitr is obligatory for every Muslim man and woman, adult and child. It should be distributed before the prayer of 'Id. Every person, having savings beyond his own and his family's feeding for one day and night should give two dollars for himself and for everyone he looks after. Zakatul Fitr is meant to purify the fasting (*saum*) and to keep everybody in society happy and pleasant — rich and poor equally — so that nobody should go hungry on that day. Thus, it presents a mangificent example of comprehensive social justice in Islam.

Sacrificial Slaughter (udhhiya):

Udhhiya or sacrificial slaughter on 'Id ul Ahda is a strongly recommended tradition. It reflects the *fact* that the Muslim being a committed, obedient servant of Allah is always ready to sacrifice anything, even his life, in Allah's way. *Udhhiya* is an imitation and remembrance of the great sacrifice that Prophet Ibrahim submitted to God by attempting to sacrifice his own son, Isma'il, to fulfil the command of Allah Almighty.

The following are the essentials of sacrifice:

i) Allah's name (Bismillahi Allahu Akbar) must be said while slaughtering.

ii) *Udhiya* cannot be slaughtered before 'Id prayer. It should be done immediately after prayers or in the three days after 'Id: Dhul hajj 11, 12, 13.

iii) *Udhhiya* can be a goat, sheep, cow, bull buffalo or camel of either sex. Pregnant female animals should not be slaughtered. Seven persons can share in the last named four animals.

iv) The meat of the slaughtered animal should be divided into three parts. It is essential to give one third as gift to the poor and the needy. One third should be given to friends and relatives and one third kept to oneself.

v) For one who intends to make the sacrificial slaughter it is sunnah not to shave his hair or clip his nails after Dhul Hajj moon is sighted, until the time of slaughter. (Sahih Muslim)

Enjoyment in 'Id Days:

Islam urges us to enjoy life with every lawful means of enjoyment. Especially on 'Id days the Islamic spirit of enjoyment and brotherhood becomes manifest. Thus Islam nourishes the spiritual aspirations of mankind along with its physical abilities.

On these days everyone should be happy with his wife, his children, his Muslim brothers and sisters. Show mutual concern by exchanging gifts, smiling on the face of each other and expressing sincere love and affection to show the bondage of *real brotherhood* which stems from the belief in Allah. All Muslims should cherish brotherly feeling in their hearts toward each other, avoid talking behind each other's backs, avoid blaming one another and avoid causing disruption in the Muslim community. These are days when we should glorify the symbols of Allah and observe His signs to have piety in our hearts.

3

PREPARATION OF THE DECEASED AND JANAZAH PRAYERS

PREPARATION OF THE DECEASED AND JANAZAH PRAYERS

PREPARATION OF THE DECEASED AND JANAZAH PRAYERS

There are five main points for the preparation of a Muslim's body for burial; we present briefly the procedure involved in each of them:

I. *Body-Washing or "Ghusl"*

Washing the deceased's body is obligatory on Muslims; it is a *Fard Kifaya*, i.e., if some members take the responsibility of doing it the need is fulfilled, but if no one fulfills it then all Muslims will be accountable.

Washing can be carried out in the following way:

1. A man's body should be washed by men and a women's by women, but a child's body may be washed by either sex. A husband can wash his wife's body and vice-versa if the need arises.

2. Only one person is needed for washing with someone to help him.

3. It is better to choose for this the person who knows best how to perform *ghusl*.

4. Place the body on a high place, e.g., a table or something similar.

5. Remove the deceased's clothes (garments) leaving the private parts covered.

6. Press the stomach gently and clean whatever comes out.

7. For washing, use a piece of cloth or your hands.

8. Only clean water may be used; add some scented oils (non-alcoholic) in the final wash. It is preferable to use warm water.

9. Perform ablution (*wudu*) for the body, cleaning the teeth and nose from outside only.

10. Wash three times, but if the body is not yet cleaned, continue washing five or seven times — it must be odd numbers.

Turn the body on its left side and begin washing the right side. Then turn it on its right side to wash the left side. This is done in each

1

wash. The first and the second washes are done with water and soap, while the last one with water and scent.

11. Hair should be unbraided, washed and combed, For women it may again be braided in three braids.

12. Dry the body with clean cloth or towel.

13. Add some perfume on the head, forehead, nose, hands, knees, eyes, armpits, and place perfumed cotton on the front and rear openings.

II. *Wrapping (Kafan)*

1. It must be a clean piece of cloth (preferably white) to cover the whole body.

2. Add some perfume to the *kafan* (non-alcoholic).

3. Do not use silk cloth for men.

4. Use three pieces for men and five for women, [but each one must cover the whole body.]

5. Tie the front and the rear with a piece of cloth (from the same *kafan*) in such a way that one can differentiate the head from the legs.

III. *Prayers (Salat)*

1. It is better that those praying divide themselves into three rows facing the *qibla* with the Imam in front.

2. Put the body (or bodies) in front of the Imam.

3. The Imam should stand by the middle of the body if the deceased is a man and by the shoulder if she is a woman.

4. If there is more than one body, then they should be put one in front of the other, those of the men nearest to the Imam and those of the women furthest from him.

5. Having the appropriate *neeyat* in your heart, raise your hands in the usual manner and say, Allahu Akbar.

6. Then fold and hold your hands on your breast in the usual manner, the right hand on the left.

7. Read *al Fatiha* quietly.

8. Say *Allahu Akbar* without raising the hands.

9. Pray for the Prophet in the same way as you do in *tashahud*.

10. Say *Allahu Akbar* (don't raise your hands).

11. Make *du'a* for the deceased.

12. Say *Allahu Akbar* (don't raise your hands).

13. Make *du'a* for the Muslims.

14. Say *Assalaamu 'Alaikum,* thus finishing the prayer.

It is clear from this description that all this prayer is done while one is standing — there is no *ruku* or *sujud* in it.

Du'a for the deceased may be chosen from the following authentic prophetic *du'as:*

اللهم اغفر له و ارحمه و عافه و اعف عنه و أكرم نزله و وسع مدخله و اغسله بالماء و الثلج و البرد و نقه من الخطايا لما نقيت الثوب الأبيض من الدنس و أبدله دارا خيرا من داره و آهلا خيرا من أهله و زوجا خيرا من زوجه و أدخله الجنة و أعذه من عذاب القبر .

اللهم اغفر لحينا و ميتنا و صغيرنا و كبيرنا و ذكرنا و انثانا و شاهدنا و غائبنا اللهم من أحييته منا فأحيه على الاسلام و من توفيته منا فتوفه على الايمان ، اللهم لا تحرمنا آجره و لا تضلنا بعده .

IV. *Funeral*

1. Procession: Mourners should walk in front or beside the bier. Those who are riding or driving should follow it.

2. Silence is recommended.

3. It is absolutely forbidden to accompany the body with music or crying.

3

V. *Burial*

1. The grave should be deep, wide and well made. It is recommended that it consist of two excavations, one inside the other. It is recommended that the smaller one called *lahd* be dug on the side of the larger one facing the qibla.

2. It is in this one that the body is put.

3. The deceased's body should be laid on the ground with the face toward the qibla, the direction of the *ka'aba*.

4. While laying it say

بسم الله وعلى ملة رسول الله .

5. It is not recommended to use a casket unless there is a need for it, e.g., if the soil is very loose or wet. A stone, or bricks or some soil should be put under the deceased's head to raise it up.

6. *Do not* use a pillow or put anything with the deceased inside the grave.

7. Cover the *lahd* with bricks so that they become like a roof for it. Pour three handfuls of soil.

8. Fill the larger pit with soil. It is preferable that each one of those present share in this by pouring three handfuls of soil. Raise the level of the grave a little less than one foot in a sloping way.

References (all in Arabic)

1. *Al Fiqh'Ala Al Madhahib Al Arab'a,* Abdul Rahman Al Jazeeri, 1970, pp. 500-535.

2. *Fiqhul Sunnah,* Vol. 4, Sayed Sabiq, 1968, pp. 69-138.

3. *Sifat Salatul Nabi,* 5th Edition, Mohammad Nasirul Deen, Al Albani, 1389 P. pp. 125.

4. *Riyadhul Saliheen,* pp. 360-373, Cairo Edition.